AGRICULTURAL MARKETING

J. W. BARKER

OXFORD UNIVERSITY PRESS

Oxford University Press, Walton Street, Oxford OX2 6DP

OXFORD LONDON GLASGOW
NEW YORK TORONTO MELBOURNE WELLINGTON
KUALA LUMPUR SINGAPORE JAKARTA HONG KONG TOKYO
DELHI BOMBAY CALCUTTA MADRAS KARACHI
NAIROBI DAR ES SALAAM CAPE TOWN

© J. W. Barker 1981
Reprinted 1983,

Published in the United States by
Oxford University Press, New York.

British Library Cataloguing in Publication Data

Barker, J W
 Agricultural marketing.
 1. Farm produce - Great Britain - Marketing
 I. Title
 630'.68'8   HD9011.5   80-41810

 ISBN 0-19-859468-2
 ISBN 0-19-859469-0 Pbk

Typeset by DMB (Typesetting), Oxford.
Printed and bound in Great Britain
by Billing and Sons Limited, Worcester

Preface

Agricultural marketing has become of particularly topical interest in recent years. During this time a great deal of publicity has been given to the desirability of agricultural producers improving their marketing skills. In 1979, this culminated in the appointment by the Minister of Agriculture, Fisheries, and Food of five experts charged with the responsibility for investigating the structure of agricultural marketing in the United Kingdom and to suggest possible improvements in efficiency.

This book is an attempt to explain some of the background to the marketing which can be practised by farmers operating under United Kingdom conditions. It considers the marketing channels which are used by farmers, both in the sales of their outputs, and in the purchases of their inputs, and anticipates likely future developments.

I am indebted to a very large number of people for their help and encouragement. For the initial inspiration to put pen to paper I will be ever grateful to the late Professor Mark Carpenter. During the course of the development of the manuscript I received assistance from many colleagues in the Faculty of Agriculture, in particular Professor Chris Ritson, Bill Cowie, Gordon Foxall, David Lesser, and Bill Weeks of the Department of Agricultural Marketing and Ken Thomson of the Department of Agricultural Economics. Peter Baron, now Professor of Agricultural Marketing at the University College of Wales, Aberystwyth also provided valuable assistance.

Additional information was given freely by a large number of people involved in the agricultural and allied industries. This applies particularly to the final section of the book dealing with the market for farm inputs. Special thanks are due to Mr Archie Sains of the Meat and Livestock Commission, Mr Jonathan Swift of the British Agricultural and Garden Machinery Dealers Association, Mr John Morley of the Central Council for Agricultural and Horticultural Co-operation and Mr A. W. Carter of the Livestock Auctioneers Market Committee.

For the preparation of the manuscript I am very grateful to Helen Campbell, Savitri Dewan, and Jude McSwaine; and for assistance with the tables Chris Lowes. Shirley Brown of the Institute of Agricultural Economics at Oxford gave invaluable help with the location of references. Finally I wish to record my gratitude to my family and friends, in particular my wife Lynne, for their continued support and encouragement. All the foregoing have assisted in the improvement of the original manuscript. For the errors which remain I accept total responsibility.

JB

Newcastle-upon-Tyne
April 1980

Contents

TO LYNNE

Introduction

Introduction

It is generally accepted that marketing is one of the most crucial aspects of farm management, and within the context of full membership of the European Economic Community (EEC) the significance of marketing in agriculture is likely to increase even further. It is also widely accepted that marketing is one of the least understood aspects of agriculture. It is the overall aim of this book to undertake a practical consideration of agricultural marketing, in order to improve, hopefully, the level of understanding.

In an attempt to make the book as meaningful and as useful as possible, it is divided into four parts. The first part examines the relevance of marketing in an agricultural environment, discussing the basic principles of marketing and the applicability of these to farming. In the light of this examination various marketing techniques applicable to farmers are considered, with particular emphasis being placed on the position of the farmer as an operator in the market. The importance of good market information is discussed, and present deficiencies in its provision are analysed.

The second part of the book considers Government legislation which has affected, and affects, the marketing of agricultural products. Particular emphasis is placed on the effect of EEC legislation. Transition to full membership of the so called 'Common Market' has involved a distinct change of emphasis in the marketing of agricultural products by UK farmers. When the EEC was founded the aim was to bring into being a vast single market for all goods, with a wide measure of common economic policies. This market included agriculture and trade in agricultural products, and hence over time Common Agricultural Policy (CAP) has been developed, and still is being developed. The practicalities of CAP are discussed, particularly the various market support systems which are now in operation.

The third part of the book considers the various marketing channels existing in agriculture which are utilized by farmers in disposing of their produce. There are various marketing channels, used throughout generations by farmers; the most important of these are considered from the point of view of their use for particular commodities. All farmers must utilize marketing channels so long as they produce goods which are in excess of their domestic consumption. For some farmers this is just a matter of routine, selling through the same channels year in and year out; however, for others it is a very important decision. All the major marketing alternatives available to farmers are considered in detail, including auctions, deadweight sales, the use of marketing boards, co-operatives, groups, contracts, and possibilities for the direct marketing of agricultural produce.

The final part of the book deals with the application of marketing principles to the purchase of farm inputs. This is a rarely considered aspect of agricultural marketing, which is perhaps surprising in view of the fact that the value of the market for agricultural inputs currently exceeds £3000 million. Although the output of the farm must inevitably account for the bulk of the farmer's marketing attention, any profits accruing to the business can be made or lost by the farmer's approach to the purchase of his inputs. Initially the size of the farmer market is considered, including some characteristics of the farmer, in order to gain an insight into the nature of the farmer as a buyer, rather than as a seller. The most important methods of distribution used to supply the farmer are also considered, and in the light of this various possibilities which exist for an orderly marketing of farm inputs are considered. Finally, consideration is given to the role of the agricultural merchant in the supply of farm inputs. Characteristics of agricultural merchants are discussed, and various trends in their function are noted.

Throughout the book likely future developments in agricultural marketing are suggested where this is applicable, and the emphasis is on the implications of agricultural marketing principles to practitioners on both sides of the farm gate.

The aim of the book is to fill a long-standing need for a book on agricultural marketing at an elementary level. It is envisaged that it will become established as recommended reading at agricultural colleges, at both county and national level. The book is also suitable for reading at a preliminary level towards university degrees in agriculture, agricultural and food marketing, and agricultural economics. It should also prove attractive to practising farmers, since the emphasis throughout is on real life applications of agricultural marketing.

Part I. Relevance of marketing in an agricultural environment

1. An introduction to marketing

Definitions of marketing

The marketing system, as it exists at present in British agriculture, is very varied. There is a combination of long standing traditional practice, compulsorily organized marketing for some products, and for others a highly complex situation from the farm gate through to the household shopping basket. Only a small minority of farmers can afford to stay in agriculture in the long term without making a profit. Thus the vast majority must be able to show some margin over expenditure in order to stay in business.

It follows from this, that, in theory at least, marketing management should be of some importance to the individual farmer, since if he is aiming to make a profit from his transactions then marketing considerations should be apparent in all of his decision making, from short term storage versus immediate sale considerations through to long-term planning of the structure of farming enterprises.

It is pertinent, therefore, to consider, at the beginning of a textbook on the marketing of agricultural products, the very nature of marketing. It is an emotive subject, with a wide range of viewpoints concerning its scope and importance. At the simplest level it might be assumed that marketing is the activity which takes place in the market. It is the collective term used to describe exchanges between buyers and sellers, who are attempting to maximize profit or subjective utility. It may be thought of quite simply as the process of making goods available for consumption. So marketing covers all business functions, including production, and in its broadest sense it covers also all production decisions. So it can be argued that, in farming, such decisions as the variety of crop to grow, or the breed of animal to keep, are marketing decisions. The concept of utility is central in marketing. The primary role of an integrated marketing system is to add form, place, time, and possession utility, so that the subjective satisfaction of consumers is maximized.

There is no universally accepted definition of marketing, indicating the variety of opinions which exist concerning the subject.

Terpstra (1972) offers a very broad definition of marketing as 'the collection of activities undertaken by the firm to relate profitability to its market'. Kempner (1976) is similarly vague. 'Marketing is the process in a society by which the demand for economic goods and services is anticipated or enlarged, and satisfied through the conception, physical distribution and exchange of such goods and services.' Hence, within any individual company which is attempting to satisfy demands of this nature, there must always be a marketing process. The success of the enterprise will depend on the ability of the management to give satisfaction and to obtain the appropriate net profit.

Kotler (1972) gives a very concise definition, in so much as 'Marketing is the set of human activities directed at facilitating and consummating exchange'. There are four major points which should be noted with regard to this definition. The first is that marketing is located specifically in the realm of human activities, in contrast to, for example, production activities which can be found in other areas of the animal kingdom. The second point is that marketing is directed at facilitating and consummating exchanges. Thus marketing covers both one-off exchanges where there is no implication of a more durable relationship, and also continuous relationships of exchange.

The third point is that the definition deliberately avoids specifying what is being exchanged. The traditional subject of exchange has been goods and services. Essentially things of value are being exchanged, and the definition is free to cover anything of value. The fourth point is that the definition deliberately avoids taking the point of view of either the buyer or seller, remaining neutral to both. Kotler suggests that there are three elements which must be present in order to define a marketing situation. These are:

(i)   Two or more parties potentially interested in exchange;
(ii) each party possesses things of value to the other(s);
(iii) each party is capable of communication and delivery.

Rodger (1971) offers a definition of marketing which is applicable to most marketing systems. 'Marketing is the primary management function, which organises and directs the aggregate of business activities involved in converting consumer purchasing power into effective demand for a specific product or service and in moving the product or service to the final customer or user so as to achieve company-set profit or other objectives.' The term 'customer', as used in this definition refers not only to the final consumer but also to intermediate market agents such as wholesalers and retailers; and in the case of farming, merchants and co-operatives and so on, who must be persuaded to purchase the product.

The term 'effective demand' implies that the price must be at a level which the customer is prepared to pay and which provides a reasonable return to the marketing agent, and the term 'specific product or service' implies that some differentiation of the product, be it by prices, promotion, or a real difference in the product itself, should be sufficient to form the basis for preference by potential customers. The definition recognizes the fact that the consumer is no longer pre-eminent in many markets, and as Galbraith (1967) has pointed out 'A large part of the management function is concerned with ameliorating the vagaries of the free market with the corporate planning which is necessary to achieve the firm's objectives'.

Agricultural marketing is often regarded by observers as having a certain associated mystique. The definition of marketing which is most applicable to agriculture is given by Kohls (1968) 'Marketing is the performance of all business activities involved in the flow of goods and services from the point of initial agricultural production until they are in the hands of the ultimate consumer.' From this definition it can be seen that groups with varying interests will view marketing differently. Consumers will be interested in purchasing what they want at the lowest possible cost, and farmers, it might be assumed, will be interested in obtaining the highest possible returns from the sale of their products. A situation such as this can result in a conflict of interests, and the continual birth and solution of such problems give marketing its essentially dynamic character. Kohls states that change is the one general rule of marketing—the status quo is never permanent.

The major reason why Kohls' definition is so particularly relevant to agricultural situations is because it can be used to determine which business activities can be properly regarded as related to marketing. The most important factor, in this respect, is the assertion that marketing can never be regarded as a neutral element by the farmer, and for this reason is worthy of his serious consideration.

It is essential to stress immediately that agricultural marketing is not a concept which is beyond the scope of the farmer. He may choose to farm in such a way that he has very few, if any, marketing decisions to make; however, his produce will still be marketed, if not by him then by a further link in the marketing chain. Changes in systems of marketing, and changes in the demand for agricultural products will eventually affect the individual and so it is in his interests to be cogniscent with, and responsive to, all aspects of agricultural marketing.

Over time marketing has been continuously developed as a management tool and this is reflected, to a certain extent, in agriculture. Kempner (1976) defines marketing management very simply as 'the engineering function in the marketing process'. The marketing manager, who in agriculture is usually the farmer himself, is responsible for the totality of a company's market offering, covering such factors as the range of products to be offered, prices charged, discounts to be offered, communications media to be employed, and the channels through which the product or service is to be made available. Marketing management is, potentially at least, present in all exchange relationships; however, it is only in recent times that marketing management has become a recognized part of industrial management.

Kotler (1972) gives a broader definition. 'Marketing management is the analysis, planning, implementation, and control of programmes designed to bring about desired exchanges with target audiences for the purpose of personal or mutual gain. It relies heavily on the adaptation and co-ordination of product, price, promotion, and place for achieving effective response.' From this it can be seen that marketing management is clearly defined as a management process and as such includes analysis, planning, implementation, and control. It is also seen as a purpose activity aimed at bringing about desired exchanges. These exchanges typically involve material goods and services, but may also involve psychological exchanges regarding organizations, persons, places, and ideas.

Thirdly, marketing management is something which can be' practised by either the buyer or the seller, whoever is seeking to stimulate the exchange process.

Fourthly, marketing management is neutral in moral content, in so much as it can be carried on for personal or for mutual gain. Marketing management is involved both with the adaptation of products and messages to existing attitudes and behaviour, and with the adjustment of attitudes and behaviour to new products and ideas.

The relative success, or otherwise, of marketing management is largely dependent on the degrees of creativity and innovation which the marketing manager contributes to the firm. An essential part of this is the appreciation of the fact that the continual vitality and growth of the firm is dependent upon delineating and fulfilling significant social and economic needs. Perhaps the most crucial reason why agriculture is placed in a unique situation with regard to marketing management is that the marketing manager, works manager, sales manager, foreman, product development manager, and shop floor workers are usually embodied in one man wearing different caps as the occasion arises, or more often perhaps family co-responsibility may be exercised.

There remains, however, the indisputable fact that marketing management is a crucial aspect of any business, however large or small it may be, and all farmers utilize the concept either consciously, or perhaps more often, unconsciously. The question remains as to whether those farmers who actively concern themselves with marketing management are any more successful than their fellows who do not—probably the most important factor is how one defines 'more successful'. If it is in financial terms alone then some fairly accurate calculations can be attempted; if qualitative factors such as happiness and peace of mind are taken into account, then the calculation becomes much more difficult.

There are therefore, a wide variety of views concerning the role of marketing in agriculture. Having suggested that fundamentally all farmers are involved in marketing, the next stage is to consider more deeply certain aspects which are of particular relevance to agriculture.

Terpstra (1972) offers a very interesting approach to marketing which can be applied, with certain qualifications, to agriculture. He identifies four tasks which must be successfully completed if a firm is to market its products properly. The first task is for the firm to study its potential customers; identifying who they are, where they are, and factors which influence their purchase or non-purchase of products. For farmers in the UK whose produce is bought by a marketing board, this task is of limited relevance. However, it is important for the majority of farmers to identify potential purchasers of their produce, with the aim of improving their understanding of the market.

The second marketing task is for the firm to develop products or services that satisfy customer needs and wants. In this regard, the firm must set prices and terms which appear reasonable to buyers, but which at the same time return what the firm considers to be a fair profit. In general, farmers are price takers rather than price setters. However, the recent increase in the importance of 'pick-your-own' enterprises on farms in the United Kingdom suggests that there is potential for farmers to develop products and services which satisfy customer needs and wants, and at the same time act as price makers.

The third task of the firm concerns the distribution function, ensuring that products are available when and where buyers can conveniently get them. This is again of relevance to farmers—it is pointless for a farmer to aim his turkey production, for example, at the fresh Christmas market, if the turkeys reach the correct weight for plucking in the middle of September. Similarly, there would be little point in growing hops in North Scotland unless the farmer was able to find some highly specialist market for the produce.

The fourth and final task of the firm is to inform the market about its produce, and this will probably include some method of persuading them to buy. For the farmer this may simply entail informing the local grain merchant of this year's tonnage which is for sale, or there may be some formal advertisement placed through the local media. A ready example of farmers utilizing persuasion to buy is seen in the British institution of paying 'luck money' to buyers, particularly of livestock. In some cases the firm's marketing responsibilities do not end with the sale. An implied warranty of satisfaction goes with the product, and thus the firm must occasionally reassure the buyer, and in many cases perform after sales services. For the farmer this may be an informal tradition, or there may be a more formalized arrangement written into, for example, a formal contract.

An examination of these four tasks illustrates that marketing involves all the activities which relate to the market. The marketing manager must plan and co-ordinate all these activities in order to produce a successul integrated marketing programme, and this applies to the farmer as much as to the businessman.

Aspects of marketing

The majority of techniques and principles can be viewed, and applied, from varying standpoints. The study of economic principles, for example, is often considered at two levels, commonly referred to as macro- and micro-economics. Macro-economics is a term originated by Frisch in 1933 (Brooman 1971) and describes the study of the aggregate performance of the whole country, and of the general price level. In contrast, micro-economics, defined by Brooman as 'the analysis of the economy's constituent elements', is concerned with the working of the markets for individual commodities, and the behaviour of the individual buyer and seller.

Marketing can similarly be studied from distinct standpoints. The two simplest, and probably most important, aspects identified are on the one hand marketing economics, which is concerned with macro-aggregate issues such as market structures, the nature and level of competition, the forms of, and reasons for, government intervention, and so on, and on the other hand marketing management, which is related largely to issues confronting individual businesses.

Within the context of this book both aspects of marketing are considered. Marketing economics is of great importance in the consideration of legislation affecting agricultural marketing, and marketing management can be applied, almost without exception, at the individual farm level. To a certain extent the two aspects are interrelated. This is inevitable; however, on the whole the distinction is helpful in providing alternative managerial and economic approaches to the problems which arise in agricultural marketing.

Orientations of businesses

There are four major orientations which can be favoured by any business, including agricultural businesses. Probably the first to develop was production orientation. The production orientated firm regards the major part of its business as being concerned with producing the goods it wishes to make. It is claimed that a significant proportion of farmers are production orientated, producing beef, for example because they always have done, and attempting to find a market for their products as and when they decide to sell. Production orientation is likely to be most successful in conditions where a sellers market exists, and the central problem to be faced by business firms is to find ways of increasing output.

The next business orientation to become dominant was financial orientation. This came about as business firms recognized that a major opportunity for profit lay in a rationalization of the industrial structure through mergers and financial consolidations. Professional bodies such as lawyers, financiers, accountants, and estate agents are particularly financially orientated, gaining ascendancy in business enterprises through skilful financial consolidation. To a certain extent all businesses are financially orientated in that if solvency is not maintained then it is only a matter of time until bankruptcy ensues.

Sales orientation was the next business orientation to become popular, as a result of there being a shortage of customers rather than a shortage of goods. The aim of sales orientation is to stimulate demand for the existing products of the firm. The tools for attempting this include increasing the advertising budget, expanding the sales force, intensifying the competition for distribution channels, and increased utilization of branding, packaging, and sales promotion. The key to sales orientation lies in merchandising and promotion used as a means of competing for a share of the existing market.

The final business orientation to develop has been marketing orientation, as a result of a realization that sales orientation does not provide the total answer for profit making in an age of rapid technological and social change, intense competition, and highly satiated consumer wants. Levitt (1962) was one of the first economists to suggest that businesses defined their operations too narrowly, being production rather than marketing orientated. He gave the now famous example of the American railroad system which at one time had been an institution in the framework of the country but which, over time, had been surpassed by road and air transport as a result of confining their operations to rail transport, rather than spanning the whole transport industry and seeking to satisfy demand—in its broadest sense—within the transport industry. The key is to define the particular needs which the firm's product fills and examine how best that need can be filled in the present and developing state of technology. If this had been done by the operators of the railways, for example, they would not have suffered competition from the airlines because they themselves would have been involved in the development of air transport.

A large number of economists came down firmly in support of the value of marketing orientated management and a considerable proportion of American companies redefined their objectives along the lines suggested by Levitt. One of the foremost supporters of this philosophy to emerge was Rodger (1971) who stated that 'the major responsibilities of general management are to establish marketing objectives' and that 'marketing is nothing more or less than the profitable matching of total company resources against market requirements and opportunities'. In other words a company should make what can profitably be sold, not make what it wants and then attempt to sell it.

It must be noted that there has not been universal acceptance of the marketing orientation principles put forward by Levitt. Heller (1972) in particular has questioned the validity of what he termed 'the myopic marketing myth'. The basic argument put forward is that much company time, money, and energy has been wasted through seeking to define the business which they are in. Thus, while Levitt's ideas have been applied on a world-wide scale in industry, it can be seen that his doctrines have not been totally accepted.

Production and marketing orientations in agriculture

The way in which farmers view their business depends very much on their personal aspirations and opinions. Two extreme positions which can be identified are those of the 'production-orientated' and the 'marketing-orientated' farmer. The production-orientated farmer regards the major part of his business as being concerned with the goods which he wishes to produce. In contrast, the marketing-orientated farmer will endeavour to produce goods which can profitably be sold, giving due consideration to the likelihood of profit before production is undertaken in the first place.

It has been stated previously that production orientation is likely to be most successful in conditions where a seller's market exists and the central problem to be faced by farmers is to find ways of increasing output. Unfortunately, in agriculture this situation very rarely arises, apart from quirks arising for climatic reasons, such as the low potato yields in Great Britain in 1975 and 1976.

The short-term nature of this situation was aptly demonstrated in following seasons.

The marketing orientation concept can be applied to agriculture to a large extent, however, to date there has been only a limited amount of work undertaken to define the orientations of farmers. Mitchell (1975) has undertaken a study of the extent to which, and the manner in which, farmers are influenced in their livestock marketing decisions by publicly-available sources of market information. He reached two general conclusions about the marketing behaviour of farmers. In general farmers' actions with regard to marketing are the result of long-term policy decisions, and as such will not be subject to review each time the farmer has occasion to sell. Also, when marketing decisions are of a short-term nature they will be influenced by many things which do not come within the purview of conventional market intelligence. Typical factors quoted as affecting sales decisions were prices, price expectations, and selling policy.

Recent work by the author[†] substantiates Mitchell's findings. In a survey of farmers throughout the United Kingdom only a small proportion appeared to regard marketing management as being of importance in their business decisions. Any marketing considerations tended to be restricted to sales decisions, with the marketing implications of purchase decisions being too long term for them to be recognized by the majority of farmers. Similarly, for management decisions, in general, production decisions were regarded as being of greater importance than marketing decisions. Production orientation was most marked among dairy farmers which is, perhaps, not surprising considering their limited marketing responsibilities.

Bateman (1972) gives a good illustration of the advantages accruing to farmers who utilize orientated management. 'Farmers essentially produce goods which satisfy consumers' demands for food. In the long term an alternative source for satisfying this demand could come from the development of synthetics. The production of orientated farmer would do little about this situation other than sit back and hope that the potential competition will not come about. The marketing orientated farmer, in contrast, would be prepared to

[†] Unpublished Ph.D. thesis entitled 'The importance of marketing management to individual farmers'. University of Newcastle-upon-Tyne.

respond to such developments. The obvious response would be for the farmer himself to investigate how far it would be possible for him to take some direct part in the development of synthetics. Although this is unlikely to be feasible there are other, more realistic, alternatives. It is possible that the development of synthetics might strengthen the demand for 'fresh farm food' unpolluted by artificial fertilizers, etc. The farmer who foresaw this and built up a reputation and a market for such produce would not suffer, but would actually benefit, from the development of synthetics'. The recent increase in the popularity of food grown using 'organic farming' methods is evidence of the potential for concentrating on a particular sector of the market.

2. Applicability of marketing principles to farmers

Approaches to agricultural marketing

Various approaches to the analysis of agricultural marketing structures have been developed. All are attempts to break down complex marketing systems into parts which can be understood more readily. One method of classifying the activities which occur in the marketing processes is to break them down into functions.

Shaw (1912), who is usually credited with the origination of this approach, defines a marketing function as 'a major specialized activity performed in accomplishing the marketing process'. One approach identifies primary and secondary functions (Kohls 1968). In this way all marketing activities are classified into three major processes, assembly, equalization, and distribution. In order to perform these principal marketing functions, various subsidiary tasks must be fulfilled, namely processing, packaging, grading or specification, transport, storage, risk bearing, demand creation price determination, financing, buying, selling, and the provision and use of market information.

The institutional approach to agricultural marketing studies the various agencies and business structures which perform the marketing processes. Marketing institutions, defined simply, are the wide variety of business organizations which have been developed to operate the marketing machinery.

To give an example of the institutional approach to food marketing, the market might be classified as follows:
A. Merchants:
  (i) Retailers;
  (ii) Wholesalers.
B. Agents:
  (i) Brokers;
  (ii) Commission Agents.
C. Speculators.
D. Processors and Manufacturers.
E. Facilitative Organizations.

Merchants hold the title to, and therefore own, the products they handle. Agents are only representatives of their clients, so they do not own the products which they handle. Speculators take title to the products with the major purpose of profiting from price movements. Processors and manufacturers exist to undertake some action on products to change their form. Facilitative organizations do not, as a general rule, participate directly in the marketing process but provide some facility to enable the process to be carried out. An example of such an organization in British agriculture would be the Meat and Livestock Commission or the Home Grown Cereals Authority.

The analytical approach to agricultural marketing problems does not attempt to describe and classify the various functions, rather it breaks down the marketing problems into their economic elements. For example, with reference to demand creation it does not describe and classify demand creation but measures demand to determine whether demand creation is necessary in the first place, or whether instead, a change in the form or the quantity of the goods is needed to meet the demand.

The analytical approach can be used as a basis for appraising any branch of agriculture, locating weak spots, and developing recommendations for improvements. A farmer appraising his livestock production, for example, would start by considering the demand for meat, whether it is increasing, decreasing, or changing in any other way over time. In particular the fluctuating demand for particular meats would be considered. Next demand would be considered with respect to place and form, for example, is lean meat in greater demand in one part of the country than in another?

The second step would be to appraise the price system for livestock and meat. This would investigate the effectiveness of prices in reflecting consumer preference to farmers and also in reflecting producers' and distributors' costs. The variability of prices would also be assessed. Again the appraisal would be in terms of time, place, and form.

The third step would be to consider the costs of marketing as such, and how they might be reduced. This includes a consideration of storage and transportation, both very relevant to all farmers. This systematic research approach provides a structural framework for appraising markets and market performance. It helps to locate the problems and state them clearly and points the way to their solution.

Basic agricultural marketing problems

The three approaches to agricultural marketing previously described have all added to the understanding of the operation of farm businesses in the United Kingdom. However, to date no analysis has been able to offer a perfect solution to three problems, basic to all farmers, which affect the marketing of their output.

The first main problem is that consumer demand for farm products is a derived demand. The utilities, or satisfactions, provided by the different farm products create the demands for them. Consumer demands are continually changing, and are exacerbated by the traditional viewpoint of farmers that their role is concluded at the farm gate and that the marketing of their produce is not their direct concern. This ties in very closely with production orientated management. It was traditionally supposed that the demand for farm products was very stable. In total, and in physical terms, it is. The total demand does not alter very much because fundamentally, the stomach is inelastic. However, the economic demand, in money value terms, varies greatly from year to year, and the demand for individual farm products varies a great deal over a number of years.

There is a traditional view that the task of the farmer is to produce those commodities which fit into his farming pattern, and from there it is the task of the merchant to find a market for the finished product. This static view of agricultural marketing is absolutely unsatisfactory, and part of the problem arises because of the dependence of a very large part of agricultural production on the weather. Climatic fluctuations can result in totally unplanned shortages and gluts of certain commodities, as has been evidenced by potato production in Great Britain in the 1970s. There are two possible reactions to this uncertainty; an offensive reaction, for example planting the right quantity of a crop assuming good conditions, or a defensive reaction, planting an acreage in excess of anticipated requirements, in case of loss due to climatic factors.

Another reason for this problem is that all agricultural production is carried out in anticipation of demand, and in certain cases the time span between an initial decision to produce and the product being ready for market can be up to 2 or 3 years. As a result it is essential that the farmer is adequately informed about marketing trends, consumer purchasing patterns, and so on *before* the decision to undertake production is made.

The most spectacular increase in demand in recent years has been that of the broiler industry. Traditionally table chickens were largely cockerels, by-products of the egg production industry; however, a latent consumer demand for a younger, smaller, more tender chicken was discovered and exploited, resulting in the growth of the broiler industry. The other striking change in demand is the shift towards more processed foods, for example, for fruits, fresh consumption per person has dropped in the UK while the consumption of some processed items has increased.

The second main problem in the field of agricultural marketing is related to the accuracy with which prices reflect consumer demands. These demands are the guides to producers as they set their production and marketing plans, and the chief medium for transmitting consumers' demands to producers is the system of market prices. When producers are able to meet consumers face to face and sell them their goods then there is no communications problem. However, agricultural production has to a certain extent become localized in specialized areas which may be many miles distant from consumers. This creates a producer-consumer communications problem, increased by the number of middlemen intervening in the marketing chain, the problem being to keep producers in touch with consumer demands and the changes which are continuously taking place in them.

The third agricultural marketing problem is concerned with getting the produce from the farmer to the consumer at the lowest cost permitted by existing technology. Marketing costs fall under the three headings of time, place, and form, including the costs of transportation from one place to another, the costs of storage from one time to another, and the costs of conversion from one form to another through processing in its broadest sense. Farmers have sometimes been dubious about the value to them of reductions in marketing costs, believing that these benefits will accrue only to the processor or distributor or, at the most, will result only in prices being held in check at the retail level. In the short term reductions in marketing costs do tend to accrue as increased profits to the section in the marketing chain which is most closely associated with the cost saving. However, in the long term the increased profits tend to be competed away and producers, distributors, and consumers all benefit.

Nature of the demand for agricultural products

The nature of the demand for agricultural production affects, to a very large extent, the applicability of marketing principles to farmers. The industry is producing food for human and animal consumption. Although every human and every animal consumes food, only a very small proportion of the total population is engaged in the purchase of agricultural products from farmers. In the United Kingdom farmers have only one buyer for all of the milk which they produce, and although a large number of firms participate in the grain trade, at the end of the day the majority of the grain trade in the western world is handled by only five firms.

It has been suggested that, given this state of the market, speculating is rather like a blind man backing horses without a form book in Braille. It has also been suggested that the demand for agricultural products is in the hands of so few, large scale purchasers that they will have the ability to manipulate the market to their advantage. Although the potential is undoubtedly there, there is little evidence that this has actually taken place up to the present time.

It is normal for a person to wish to eat until his appetite is completely satisfied. If his income is so low that he cannot afford his desired level of food consumption, any increase in income is likely to be spent mainly on extra food. On the other hand, at high levels of income, food consumption becomes a less important factor in the individual's budget, and any increase in income will not lead to an increase in the quantity of food produced, although it may result in extra expenditure through the purchase of better quality food. A relationship between food consumption and the price charged has also been established, and a generalized concept has been devised to identify the relationship. Almost invariably lower prices are necessary to bring about increased consumption of a good or service. The extent to which consumption responds to changes in prices varies between commodities. The concept of price elasticity of demand can be used to measure the extent of the response, and can be defined as the percentage change in demand for a commodity as a result of a given small percentage change in the price of that same commodity.

So price elasticity = percentage change in quantity demanded ÷ percentage change in price of demand

(all relating to a particular good or service)

For a 1 per cent change in price of a good or service, if the quantity demanded changes by more than 1 per cent, demand for the good or service is said to be elastic (or highly responsive to changes in price), if the quantity demanded changes by less than 1 per cent demand is said to be inelastic.

There is a definite relationship between the price elasticity of demand for a product and the total revenue to be derived from production. With elastic demand, as output increases, so does total revenue, and with inelastic demand as output is increased, total revenue is reduced. The implication of this is that producers facing an inelastic demand for their product have little incentive to increase their output. As will be discussed later, this is of great relevance in agriculture.

There are various factors which determine the nature of the price elasticity of demand for a good or service, perhaps the most important being the availability of substitutes. The better the substitute the greater will be the elasticity of demand. So, for food as a commodity, demand is relatively inelastic because there is no acceptable substitute, apart from synthetic products to a certain extent. However, competition between different types of food is much more intense, and so demand is much more elastic. Time is also an important factor, allowing substitutes to be devised and improved, therefore demand is more elastic in the long than in the short term.

Income elasticity of demand relates the resonsiveness of demand to changes in consumers' income and can be defined as the percentage change in the demand for a commodity as a result of a given small percentage change in the incomes of consumers.

Income elasticity of demand = percentage change in quantity demanded ÷ percentage change in incomes of consumers.

For most goods income elasticity of demand is positive, with an increase in income leading to an increase in quantity demanded. On the other hand if an item is regarded as inferior, an increase in income brings about a decrease in consumption, and income elasticity is negative. If demand is inelastic then the industry will be stagnant; as incomes rise, any increase in disposable income will be spent on other goods. Where demand is elastic, an increase in income will lead to a greater than proportional increase in consumption of the goods, and the industry will be buoyant.

Engel, a nineteenth century German statistician, observed that over time expenditure on food, as a proportion of total expenditure, declines as income increases. Engel's Law, as it has become known, implies that the income elasticity of demand for food will decline as incomes increase. Engel also suggested that as incomes increase, a greater proportion of disposable income will be spent on 'luxuries' such as recreation, and convenience and leisure goods. This can be viewed graphically as in Fig. 2.1.

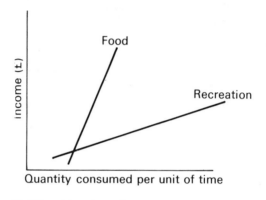

Fig. 2.1. Graphical illustration of Engel's Law.

As incomes increase, the quantity of food consumed increases, but only by a small amount, since the income elasticity of demand for food is low. In the Western world at the present time, with high average household incomes, the demand for virtually all agricultural products is inelastic.

Income elasticity of demand can be used to refer to either a change in expenditure or a change in quantity consumed as related to changes in income. These two elasticities are not necessarily the same. Since the Second World War expenditure on food has risen to a much greater extent than quantity consumed per capita. Much of this increase in food expenditure comes about as a result of the purchase of more services with food. A quick glance in the food department of any modern supermarket confirms this, with meat offered prepacked in polythene and polystyrene and chilled in refrigerators, bread sliced and wrapped, and cakes and sweets provided in a multitude of foil and paper wrappings, and cardboard boxes. This results in an increased expenditure on food items, but does not necessarily mean that more pounds, or calories, of food are being consumed.

Fox (1951) undertook a study of the effect of price and income changes on consumption, and determined income elasticity of demand on the basis of both expenditure and quantity purchased. For 1948 he found the income elasticity of demand for all food expenditures in the USA to be 0.42. Dividing this into expenditure for food at home and expenditure in restaurants, he found income elasticity at home to be 0.29, while the income elasticity for expenditures away from home was 1.14. This ties in with the current situation in Great Britain where, as incomes have risen, people have shown an increasing propensity to eat out.

In Great Britain an estimate of the price and income elasticities of demand for all major food-stuffs is given by the National Food Survey. This began in July 1940 as a check on the nutritional standards of diets under wartime food rationing. Originally it was confined to urban working-class households, but in 1950 it was extended to all classes of households. The survey is based on a random sample of households, and is continuous. The results are unlikely to be totally accurate, in particular because the survey omits any food bought and consumed away from the house. However, the annual reports in the Household Food Consumption and Expenditure Series provide a major source of information concerning the nature of the demand for the foods produced by the farmer.

Table 2.1 gives the latest available values of the price and income elasticities of demand for various food commodities.

Supply position of the farmer

Various factors have an important influence on the supply position of the individual farmer. The most important of these include:

1. *Discontinuity of supply*

The production of most agricultural commodities, especially arable crops, is seasonal in nature. For some, storage is possible, so long

Table 2.1. Elasticities of demand for selected food
commodities in 1978

| Commodity | Income elasticity of demand[†] | | Price elasticity of demand |
	By expenditure	By quantity purchased	
Liquid milk	0.03[‡]	0.02	−0.16
Cream	1.16[‡]	0.96	−0.80
Beef and veal	0.37	0.29	−1.37
Mutton and lamb	0.44	0.43	−0.94
Pork	0.24	0.20	−1.65
Eggs	0.03	−0.01	−0.09
Butter	0.13	0.13	−0.33
Margarine	−0.20[§]	−0.25	+0.65[‖]
Sugar	−0.08	−0.12	−0.51
Fresh potatoes	−0.16	−0.23[¶]	−0.17
Fresh green vegetables	0.22	0.14 e.g. cabbages	−0.42
Other vegetables	0.42	0.26 e.g. root vegetables	−0.78
Fresh fruit	0.50	0.47 e.g. apples	−0.42
Bread	−0.03	−0.08	−0.54
All food	0.21		

[†] In general, the income elasticity of demand for food is greater by expenditure than by quantity purchased.
[‡] There is a notable difference between the income elasticities of demand for milk and cream. Milk is regarded as a basic product and therefore consumption does not vary according to income to any great extent. In contrast, the elasticity for cream is much greater since it is regarded as a luxury product.
[§] Margarine is regarded as an inferior product (with respect to butter) and so has a negative income elasticity of demand. As incomes rise, people are more able to afford to luxury products, and increase their consumption of butter, at the expense of margarine.
[‖] The price elasticity of demand given for margarine is its cross price elasticity of demand with respect to butter.
[¶] For fresh potatoes, as incomes rise consumers begin to buy services such as pre-packed and/or washed potatoes, frozen chips and so on. So income elasticity of demand by expenditure is greater than by quantity purchased.

Source: MAFF (1980).

as space is available, but for other products there is the added problem of perishability. A livestock farmer, for example, can take his cattle home from market, within certain limits, if he is not satisfied with the price he is offered. However, if a tomato producer employed similar tactics, he would be left with a consignment of overripe produce, worth virtually nothing.

In all of agriculture discontinuity of supply is a problem, making it difficult for the farmer to establish regular outlets, and making it a feasible notion that planned and co-ordinated marketing should result in improved returns to production.

2. *Small quantity production*

Farms differ from industrial firms in that they are comparatively small businesses, unable to easily co-ordinate their production with other producers, and without hope of singly financing a marketing programme from their possible level of output. Having said that, although the individual farmer is not in a position to mount an advertising campaign for his production, his scale is sufficient to merit the drawing up of plans and objectives, even if these are only on the back of a cigarette pack, or kept within the head.

3. *Nature of agricultural products*

The nature of agricultural products is peculiar in that, by and large, the output of agriculture is for intermediate rather than final consumption. This discounts the proportion of agricultural products which is sold at the farm gate. The intermediate nature of agricultural production reduces the ability of the farmer to take his share of the marketing margin, and makes him dependent on factors in addition to retail conditions.

As was mentioned earlier, agricultural products are more perishable than their industrial counterparts, and they are also bulky in character. This creates problems of transport; in general unit costs of transport are higher in agriculture than in industry.

4. *Agricultural market conditions*

Two major aspects of agricultural markets particularly affect farmers. The first aspect is the static nature of the market. In industry a general feature of markets is that the innovator is usually well placed to reap speculative profits until rival firms catch up with the new techniques adopted by the market leader. A good example in 1978, in the sports goods and toys field, was the innovation of the skateboard. In agriculture there is much less facility for the individual producer to innovate, other than to adopt existing production processes. The individual usually has neither the scale, nor the available capital to increase his share of the market through innovation. The slow rate of acceptance of boar pork and bull beef is an example of the limiting factors facing agricultural innovators.

Another aspect of market conditions which is peculiar to the agricultural industry is the degree of price support which has been, and still is, offered to producers. In the United Kingdom over the last 40 years the farmer has had, by one means or another, a supported market, in that the Government has controlled prices, giving producers a certain minimum return. Initially this support was through deficiency payment schemes and legislation introducing marketing boards for certain commodities, and latterly there has been a transition to the EEC Common Agricultural Policy with minimum import prices, intervention buying, and so on.

The actual mechanics of market support are discussed in more depth in Part B; however, the net result as far as the farmer is concerned is that he is operating in an environment which greatly reduces his marketing responsibility. Agricultural marketing differs from commercial marketing because in some ways the farmer does not face by any means as keen a competitive climate as that in industry. For most commodities, the farmer has a reasonably assured market at a reasonably assured price. It follows, therefore, that he will rate production considerations to be of paramount importance, grumbling only when 'the Government' allow prices to drop below the level at which he would prefer to sell. There is therefore less incentive for the farmer to market aggressively. At worst there is always a bottom to the market for most commodities, something which rarely exists in other industries. Because of the market support measures, in practice the price system for agricultural products does not work freely in the United Kingdom. In many cases there is direct interference by the Government for political and welfare reasons, and in other cases the price differentials that consumers pay or would be willing to pay for different qualities of a product are not reflected fully through the marketing system to producers, being narrowed down or eliminated on the way.

Much of this problem is related to the nature of the supply of agricultural products. In the short term agricultural production is relatively fixed, so that if prices rise for a certain type of livestock, as a result of an increase in demand, it is physically impossible for farmers to *immediately* increase their supplies of the particular commodity. This fixity of supply is shown graphically in Fig. 2.2.

In the short term, an increase in demand for livestock will result in an increase in price from OP to OP_1. However, producers cannot immediately respond with additional production, and so it can be said that their price elasticity of supply, the response of supply to a change in the price of a commodity, is zero.

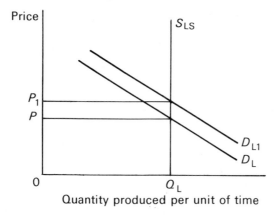

Fig. 2.2. Short-term supply position of farmers.

In the long term it is obviously possible to increase supply, beef breeding herds can be increased for example, and in all cases farmers have an opportunity to adjust their production levels. The long term situation is seen in Fig. 2.3.

Over time, production is increased, from QLS to QLL, and this may result in a reduction of prices from OP_1 to OP_2. So in the long term the elasticity of supply is more than zero, and in agriculture long term supply responses are usually very elastic in response to price changes. This is very closely related to a paradox which exists with regard to the nature of the demand for agricultural products.

Since the demand for food is inelastic at the macro level, there is no incentive for total production to be increased, since this will result in a reduction in total revenue. However, within limits, individual producers are producing against a perfectly elastic demand curve, since their scale of operation is too small to influence the total market directly. It is only in the long term that the consequences of changes in production levels are translated back to the farmer through the price system. So for milk production in the United Kingdom, given the nature of the market for milk, there are no demand restrictions on the output of the individual producer. However, if all farmers decided to increase production this would have a very large effect on total milk supplies.

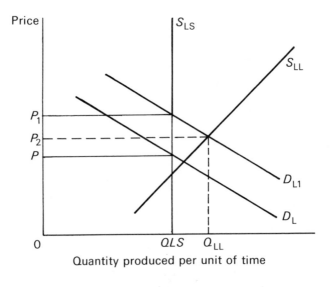

Fig. 2.3. Long-term supply position of farmers.

Long-term trends in agricultural production

In United Kingdom agriculture, there has been an average increase in per capita production of almost 2 per cent per annum over the last 100 years. This is a result of a combination of circumstances, including better working conditions, more and better capital equipment, improved genetic potential in livestock and cereals, and a replacement of man and horse power by more efficient machinery. The increases in production have not been constant over time, however.

Regular fluctuations or cycles in aggregate output and prices have been observed for many agricultural commodities in Great Britain and in other countries. The production and price cycles are related systematically as periods of abnormally high production and low prices alternate with periods of low production and high prices. The length of the cycle, which is not rigidly fixed, appears to be in some way related to the duration of the natural production cycle for the commodity concerned. The movements are generally referred to as cycles. This is perhaps an over generalization, implying a more fixed, regular periodicity than the movements actually show. Oscillations is perhaps a more accurate description.

Cyclical behaviour is largely a result of incorrect future expectations by producers. A producer may anticipate future high prices for a particular product, and so increase the production of that commodity on his farm. Other producers may have similar expectations and also increase production. Because of this, production may be higher than anticipated when the time comes to sell the product, and as a result, the actual price received may be much lower than expected. This lower price is likely to result in pessimistic future opinions concerning the commodity, and production may be reduced. As a result of this, prices would rise again.

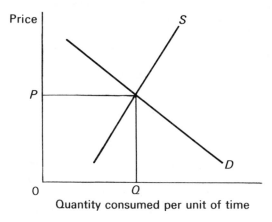

Fig. 2.4. Determination of equilibrium price, aggregate supply, and aggregate demand.

Theoretical analysis of cycles such as this has frequently been based on the Cobweb Theorem, introduced by Ezekiel (1938). The simple law of supply and demand explains how aggregate supply, aggregate demand, and the equilibrium market price are determined simultaneously, as shown in Fig. 2.4.

Aggregate supply and demand equate at only one point, with an output of OQ, at the equilibrium market price of OP.

Cobweb analysis differs from static neo-classical theory in that it allows for a time lag between the decision to produce and the decision to sell. This is particularly appropriate to agriculture, where there are frequent time lags between price changes and adjustments in supply, due to the length and inflexibility of the production period.

The problem is that it may take as long as 2 or 3 years for production to be adjusted to changes in the equilibrium situation. However, market prices will have adjusted immediately. The difference between this and the simple equilibrium cases results fundamentally from the time lag; other contributory factors include the fact that farmers are influenced more heavily by current prices than by suggested prospective market conditions. The paradox between the price elasticity of demand for agricultural products between the individual producer and total output is also relevant, since because each individual producers' output is so small he will ignore the effect of marginal increases in his output on total production. However, if enough producers think in this way, there is a snowball effect on output.

There are three possible long-term Cobweb situations, which one is applicable depending on the relative balance between the elasticities of supply and demand for the commodity. The three situations are illustrated in Fig. 2.5.

The equilibrium position is an output, OQ, and market price, OP. However, although farmers can plan towards a certain output of a commodity, there is no guarantee that this output will be achieved. A disease problem, for example, could result in a reduced output of OQ_1. Because of this shortfall in supply, prices will rise to OP_1. Any farmers basing future production on this price will plan to increase output; in aggregate they will plan an output of OQ_2. However the appropriate price for this level of production is OP_2. The natural reaction to this low price would reduce production, in aggregate to OQ_3. The response of market price to this would be to rise to OP_3. This fluctuation is likely to continue over time.

The long-term situation depends on the price elasticities of supply and demand. If supply is less elastic than demand, that is less responsive to change in price, then a convergent Cobweb results, eventually returning to equilibrium conditions. If supply is

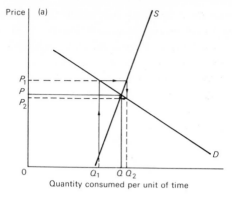

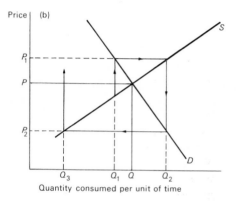

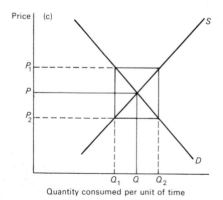

Fig. 2.5. Possible cobweb situations. (a) Convergent or stable cobweb. (b) Divergent or explosive cobweb. (c) Perfect or continuous cobweb.

more elastic than demand, so that supply is more responsive to changes in price, then a divergent Cobweb results with violent fluctuations in output. A continuous Cobweb arises if the elasticities of supply and demand are in balance.

There are various examples of Cobweb-type fluctuations in agriculture. The most publicized is the pig cycle, with prices fluctuating roughly over a 2 year period. When prices are at a peak production is increased resulting in extra supply and lower prices, then production is reduced, prices rise again, and so on. Allen (1958) has identified a pig cycle of 2-3 years duration in the United Kingdom and a potato cycle of 3-5 years duration.

It has been suggested that in recent years the cyclical movements have speeded up, mainly as a result of improved market information and communications and improved production techniques. It has also been suggested that, as a result of the large scale investment now required to undertake the production of most agricultural commodities efficiently, farmers will be less able to jump in and out of production in response to changes in price. However, there is, in practice, little evidence of any reduction in the extent of cyclical fluctuations.

Other agricultural commodities for which fluctuations are commonplace include eggs, turkeys, beef, and wheat. All come about as a result of mistaken future expectations, and it is a sad fact that an industry which has undergone a massive transformation in its production techniques still bases production decisions on whims and fancies, although this is inevitable given the lack of accurate, and easily understandable market information relating to future market conditions.

Agriculture is in a position where the price elasticity of supply is much greater than the price elasticity of demand, hence there is potentially a divergent Cobweb situation. This is one of the basic reasons for Government market support to stabilize the production system. Traditionally the guaranteed price scheme has been used in the United Kingdom, and now Common Agricultural Policy provides guaranteed intervention prices and the like. Their effect is shown graphically in Fig. 2.6.

Under these conditions there continues to be a fluctuation of prices and production. However, production is trapped in a continuous oscillation (*ABCD*). This makes the setting of the guaran-

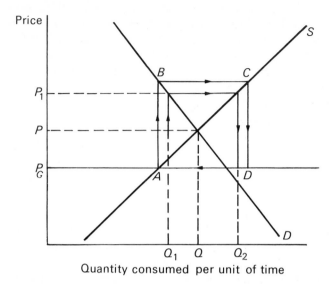

Fig. 2.6. Effect of Government setting prices for agricltural commodities.

teed price, or intervention price, (P_G) of crucial importance. It should be set as near to the equilibrium price (P) as possible.

If the intervention price is set below the equilibrium price, then output purchased during periods of low prices and high production can be stored and sold during times of low supplies and high prices. By this method losses of production are reduced. However, if there is a miscalculation and prices are set at above the equilibrium price, consistent overproduction occurs, with no opportunity for disposal of the surplus production within the community. This results in the famous 'mountain' stockpiles of commodities and the need to offload produce outside the community.

It must be noted that the principles put forward by Ezekiel concerning cyclical fluctuations in agriculture have not been universally accepted. Critics of Cobweb theory maintain that in the real world the variability of agricultural prices with time is irregular, not regular as was supposed by Ezekiel. Cochrane (1958) suggests that the irregular price variability is due to three factors, which over time break down the cobweb. These factors are changes in demand, technical innovations, and deviations between intended output and actual output.

He has also constructed synthetic Cobweb models for potatoes, pigs, and milk based on empirical estimates of the elasticities of demand and supply for these products in the United States. The price and production cycles which were generated by these models were then compared with the paths traced out by co-ordinates of prices received in one period and actual production in the following period, over several years. For each of the three commodities examined the actual price-output path was quite irregular and bore little or no resemblance to the idealized Cobweb model.

There are two other major criticisms of Cobweb theory. The first is that it does not allow for price uncertainty, which of course does occur in British agriculture. The second criticism is that whereas the theory implies a cycle with a duration of two production periods, empirical observations suggest a cycle length of four production periods for pigs and other agricultural products. McClements (1970) has met this objection by modifying the simple Cobweb model to include a partial adjustment hypothesis. In any one production period, planned supply is adjusted by a fixed proportion of the difference between intended output for the current period and actual output in the previous period. Despite its shortcomings, the Cobweb theorem does provide a testable hypothesis concerning the mechanism of agricultural supply response, and modification of the simple model to include the partial adjustment hypothesis greatly adds to its flexibility.

Marketing position of the farmer

It is highly desirable that the price mechanism should operate smoothly and accurately in agriculture so that farmers can obtain an accurate reflection of what consumers want, when they want it, and in what particular form. It is in this sense that the economics of marketing does not merely begin at the farm gate and end at the supermarket. It begins long before that, when farmers decide which varieties of cereals to plant, or the breeds of livestock to rear, and in what quantities, in the light of consumer demands and their own abilities to produce. This continues throughout production, involving questions of on-farm storage in the case of crops, and weight and finish in the case of livestock. Thus, in its full sense, agricultural marketing is much more than simply selling farm produce.

However, because of the unusual supply and demand conditions under which the individual farmer operates, in general he is unable to fully apply marketing principles to his business transactions. In fact, it is possible to exist in agriculture without any concern for marketing at all. With reference to the market orientation concept previously discussed, the truly production-orientated livestock farmer will, perhaps, stock up with the same numbers and types of store cattle every year as his grass grows, accepting the price he has to pay, usually with a grumble. He will then wait for them to grow and reach some standard level of fatness in their own good time, once more accepting the price he receives at the time of sale, invariably with even louder grumbles! He will be involved with no direct marketing effort and will probably survive so long as he is lucky enough to have land in good heart, and no immediate prospects of handing over the farm to his son to worry about.

The majority of farmers are much more market orientated than that. However, having said that most farmers are still production orientated to the extent that they would never seriously contemplate giving up and investing their capital outside farming, unless, sadly, they are faced with no alternative.

There is great confusion, in agriculture generally, between selling and marketing. Many farmers regard themselves as being 'marketing orientated' simply because they attend a number of local auction markets. Kaddar (1975) gave a good identification of the essential difference between selling and marketing. Selling he sees as the function in the marketplace, where the salesman tries to dispose of the available produce for the best price which the customer is willing to pay. Marketing, in contrast, is much more comprehensive and aims at maximizing the returns to the producer, at a price the consumer can afford. Marketing starts with production and continues through every facet of the distribution channel until the consumer finally purchases the produce.

Kaddar further claims that only a few farmers understand the necessity of producing to meet the market, and finding a market for their produce. His solution for this dilemma is to encourage the growth of co-operatives to undertake the marketing responsibility for the individual. This suggests that most farmers are basically production orientated, and make very little application of marketing principles in their business management. The situation is probably not quite so extreme as that in actual practice. Viaene

(1977) identifies three new trends in the marketing of agricultural products by farmers. These are:

(i)   Direct marketing to the consumer, by-passing the middle men and reducing costs.
(ii) Contract production, benefiting both producers and buyers, the farmer receiving guarantees on finance and prices, thus reducing risks, and the buyer being assured of quality, quantity, and time of delivery.
(iii) Marketing through co-operatives, with farmers tending to improve their bargaining power.

All of these trends will be discussed in greater depth in later chapters, however, the general conclusion still remains that in agriculture the application of marketing principles is limited to a very great extent.

3. Applicability of marketing techniques to farmers

Marketing mix

In the previous chapter various principal and subsidiary marketing functions were identified as being of relevance to a firm in the disposal of its output. In different industries, and for different firms, the relevance of particular functions will vary. To a certain extent all firms will fulfil functions such as packaging and demand creation in a specific way. The key concept here is that of the marketing mix, defined by Kotler (1972), as 'the set of controllable variables that the firm can use to influence the buyers' responses'.

There are a large number of variables which qualify for inclusion in the marketing mix. McCarthy (1971) introduced a four-factor classification popularly known as the 'four Ps'—product, place, promotion, and price, and each classification includes a number of marketing considerations, as shown in Table 3.1. The marketing mix is regarded by many firms as being of very great importance, and marketing programmes are designed specifically to determine the optimal marketing mix.

Table 3.1. Elements of the marketing mix

Product	Place	Promotion	Price
Quality	Distribution channels	Advertising	Level
Features and options	Distribution coverage	Personal selling	Discounts and
Style	Outlet locations	Sales promotion	allowance
Brand name	Sales territories	Publicity	Payment terms
Grading	Inventory levels		
Packaging	Transportation		
Product line	Market information		
Warranty			
Service level			
Other services			
Market research			

Within this chapter five marketing techniques, all elements of the marketing mix, are examined in depth with relation to their applicability to the farmer, and observations are made concerning how far such techniques can, and should, be used by the farmer. The five techniques which will be considered are advertising, market research, pricing, grading, and the provision and use of market information. This group, whilst not exhaustive, is representative of the elements comprising the marketing mix.

Applicability of advertising

Advertising is generally accepted as being one of the most important activities by which the firm conveys persuasive communications to its target buyers. It is normally identified as consisting of non-personal forms of communication conducted through paid media under clear sponsorship. Colley (1961) defines advertising as 'mass paid communication, the ultimate purpose of which is to impart information, develop attitudes, and induce action beneficial to the advertiser'.

Advertising expenditure in Great Britain has increased steadily as the nation progressed from the early days of the Industrial Revolution to the acquisitive and affluent society in which we live today. Although Dr Johnson contended in 1759 (Turner 1968) that 'advertisements are now so very numerous that they are very negligently perused', over two centuries later advertisements are so attractively presented that they are perused more avidly than ever. It is questionable whether all the expenditure on advertising is justified. As Lord Leverhulme once pointedly remarked 'Probably half of every advertisement appropriation is wasted—but nobody knows which half'. Increasingly some advertisers appear to be motivated by the maxim that so long as the product sells, nothing else matters. In a very revealing article about aphrodisiacs, Hughes (1969) once commented 'Whatever else it achieves, it certainly seems to be stimulating sales'.

Most individual farmers produce on too small a scale to justify mounting a large scale advertising campaign when promoting their sales. Farmers do however use informal advertising, usually at a local level. The simplest form of advertising which a farmer can use is word of mouth contact with known potential buyers. Similarly a farmer can advertise the fact that he wishes to sell some corn by contacting a number of merchants personally, letting them have samples, and then seeing what prices they will offer. It is possible for this type of advertising to be formalized using local newspapers.

When farmers act in unison, their potential for advertising is much increased, with the costs being shared among a large number of producers. This may be through a farmers marketing co-operative, or it may take the form of generic advertising at the commodity level. One of the best examples in Great Britain of a national advertising campaign undertaken for, and on behalf of, farmers, and paid for by them, is the meat advertising undertaken by the Meat Promotion Executive. This body was set up at the request of the National Farmers Union in an attempt to improve the competitive position of home produced meat by means of national advertising campaigns. The budget available to the Meat Promotion Executive has been consistently expanded and is financed by means of a levy imposed on cattle, sheep, and pigs, the cost of the levy being divided equally between the buyer and the seller of the livestock at the point of slaughter.

The advertising policy has been mainly concentrated on in-store promotions and television campaigns featuring well-known personalities, and has met with considerable criticism. In particular, it has been adversely compared with the campaigns of competing importers. This criticism will probably remain valid so long as British meat is not supported by a consistent brand image, such as that enjoyed by 'Danish Bacon' and 'New Zealand Lamb'.

The other two major advertising campaigns for agricultural commodities in the United Kingdom are for eggs and milk. The Eggs Authority undertake a great deal of general advertising of eggs, on behalf of egg producers, in an attempt to stimulate demand. Campaigns have included 'go to work on an egg', 'see what an extra duz does', and so on. The promotion is financed from a levy paid to the Eggs Authority by egg producers. It is worth noting in passing that in the 1960s the British Egg Marketing Board, which was then responsible for the marketing of eggs produced in the United Kingdom suffered the adverse effects of having an unfavourable brand image created for their products. All eggs passing through a packing station were stamped, primarily to prevent the Government subsidy to egg producers being paid twice. Commodity advertising was based on the 'little lion' emblem incorporated in the stamp. The lion stamp quickly became associated, however, not with quality, but with lack of quality, in particular a lack of freshness. This resulted in a decline in the demand for stamped eggs, and in part to the demise of the British Eggs Marketing Board.

The advertising of milk in Britain is undertaken primarily through the marketing boards which represent all milk producers in the country. The Milk Publicity or Dairy Councils, the Milk Marketing Boards, and the dairymen join forces in presenting milk and its products to the public. The councils concentrate their efforts on national advertising, educational media, and publicity material. The funds for these activities are contributed by milk producers and the dairymen. Additionally milk producers finance the promotional work of their Boards, and the Boards also contribute funds to bodies publicizing cheese and butter. In 1977-78 the Boards spent £10m on advertising and sales promotion, which was equal to 0.068 pence per litre of milk sold from farms. Well known slogans incorporated in milk advertising have included 'Drinka Pinta Milka Day' and 'Pick up a Pint and stay on top'. The Board also undertake more broadly-based sponsorship, designed to promote the image of milk, in particular an annual national cycle race, widely known as the Milk Race. Funds made available by the EEC's Co-responsibility levy on milk production have also been used to promote the consumption of milk and milk products in the United Kingdom.

Although generic advertising has been used to a large extent in agriculture it is difficult to demonstrate its success in sales promotion. Over time criticisms have been made about the appropriateness of the technique and May (1977) identifies five major problems which are inherent in the nature of generic advertising, and which weakens its effectiveness. These five factors are quality control, quantity control, the structure of the market, the organizational structure of the body concerned with undertaking the campaign, and the timing of the campaign. So, although generic advertising is widely applied, its success is not absolute. It must be said, however, that as a result of an econometric analysis, May found that generic advertising had a substantial and statistically significant positive effect on per capita consumption of eggs in the United Kingdom over the time period 1956-76.

Applicability of market research

Market research is a technique which has now been almost universally accepted by firms throughout industry. It is designed to give decision makers further information about problems and opportunity areas. In order to achieve this, market research can include a wide variety of techniques, such as market surveys, product preference tests, sales forecasting by region, and advertising effectiveness studies.

Formal market research has been carried out only for the last 60 years and over this time there has been an acceleration in the number of firms setting up departments within their structure with a responsibility for market research. Specialist market-research firms have also been instituted undertaking, for a fee, market research services for clients. There is a great deal of scope for market research in industry, so long as it fulfils its aim, because the successful firm is likely to be the one which is most accurately informed about the future prospects of the market in which it deals.

There are various reasons for the increasing popularity of market research, one of the most important probably being that with mass production aimed at a mass market, individual customers are unknown to the producer. Market research is one way of getting to know more about the customer. Also, partly as a result of inflation and the increased bargaining power of trade unions, the market for most goods has expanded vastly, now including people who could not afford the products previously. The requirements of such customers may well be different to those of the existing clientele, and it is the place of market research to afford information concerning the nature of the expanding market.

In farming, the scope for market research exists to a similar extent as in industry. It would be folly, however, to suggest that an individual farmer can justify having a separately staffed market-research department within his management team, unless he is operating on an exceptionally large scale. In general the farmer will not have the turnover to justify undertaking formal market research, although, this does not mean that farmers cannot, and do not, benefit from the provision of market research undertaken on their behalf. In fact, a wealth of market research is undertaken for farmers, the results of which are to a certain extent indigestible so far as the farmer is concerned, and to a large measure undigested.

At the level of the individual farm, it is essential that all farmers undertake a certain amount of their own market research, so that they can be continually aware of market opportunities which might arise. This becomes particularly important if the farmer is planning a change of farming systems, and there are a wide variety of planning techniques which can be utilized to this end.

At the national level in the United Kingdom the Government accepts responsibility for the provision of market research and advice. The bulk of this work is undertaken by the Ministry of Agriculture, Fisheries, and Food, through their agencies, and also by University faculties of Agriculture, and other national agricultural bodies. The following two examples of the use of market research in British agriculture suggest possible applications of the concept to the farmer.

One example is the Agricultural Development and Advisory Service (ADAS) arm of the Ministry of Agriculture which undertakes a great deal of market research, both for farmers in general, and for individual farmers upon demand. For example, if a farmer was contemplating a major change in farming policy, such as changing from dairying to arable farming, a local ADAS official would undertake a full study of the situation—utilizing practical market research—including an investigation of whether the change would qualify for financial assistance through any of the Government's financial assistance schemes then in force.

A second example is the work of the Central Council for Agricultural and Horticultural Co-operation (CCAHC). This is a Government initiated and financed body charged with the aim of helping farmers and growers throughout the UK to cut costs, increase profits, and create market opportunities through working more closely together on one or more parts of their business.

Upon demand the CCAHC will undertake a wide range of studies for farmers, reviewing the potential for co-operation in various types of joint venture, for example a central grain-storage scheme, or concerted marketing of seed potatoes. In this way practical market research is undertaken for the farmer, with future market conditions being reviewed by the Central Council officer.

Applicability of pricing

Pricing is regarded as an essential element of the marketing mix by the majority of economists, and although recently there has been a divergence of opinion over its relative importance, few, if any marketeers would regard it as being of no importance. Pricing is certainly important when a new product is being introduced to the market; the price which is charged may mean the difference between a successful or an unsuccessful product launch.

The extent of discretion in pricing which the seller will have available to him will depend on the nature of the product. If a product is identical to others then the seller will have no price discretion at all, but if it is very different to other products the marketing executive will have very large discretion over the price which should be charged. Various techniques of pricing have been developed over time, including cost-orientated pricing which adds a fixed margin or percentage to the cost of production. This does not take the market into account at all, and is therefore a short-sighted method of pricing. An alternative is target pricing which is also cost based, setting the price at a level which is considered to give sufficient returns to cover costs and leave a reasonable profit.

Demand-orientated pricing sets a high price for a product when demand is high, and a low price when demand is weak. Price differentiation can be achieved by slight product variation, or price discrimination, based upon market segmentation. With competition-orientated pricing, prices are maintained in relation to the price of competitors. If the nature of the market is not well understood, this may lead to market disruptions at times.

The alternative pricing possibilities are of limited relevance to the farmer. His ability to act as a price setter is usually very restricted. He is much more likely, and also much more accustomed, to be in a position of accepting prices which are set by the market, usually heavily influenced by a few large buyers. Although the farmer is a past master at the art of bartering, this will cover only the marginal penny or pound on the final price. With regard to overall pricing, the farmer has very little control.

Taking the example of the milk producer, the British farmer will have no influence whatsoever on the price of his product, since the prices are set by Government edict and administered by the Milk Marketing Board. All the farmer can do is attempt to improve the quality of his product to qualify for higher payments. He might attempt also to increase the quantity of his production because there is no disincentive for overproduction.

In all of agricultural production the potential of the individual farmer to administer prices is very limited, the greatest potential for improving and influencing the price received by farmers coming from co-operative action with a number of farmers acting in unison. It is a basic business principle that as firms increase their share of the market, then their influence on the market will increase correspondingly. This holds in farming, and various farmers co-operatives have been introduced, in Great Britain and throughout the world, with the aim of improving the competitive position of the farmer members. This particular aspect of agricultural marketing will be considered in greater detail in Chapter 8.

Applicability of grading

Agricultural output is typically heterogeneous in quality, as a result of a number of factors, including differences in breed varieties, different cultural practices, and the effects of weather, location, and disease. Grading is the process of segregating such a heterogeneous supply into smaller, more homogeneous groups. The homogeneity will be in respect to specified quality characteristics, and in practice there must always be a compromise between minimizing variations within grades and the cost of establishing the variation of each grade.

Grading can be of benefit to both the farmer and to consumers of agricultural products. Consumers can increase their satisfaction by obtaining with certainty the particular qualities they prefer, to the exclusion of those they do not desire, and farmers can, potentially, increase their returns by taking the maximum advantage of buyers' quality preferences. In addition to these fundamental advantages of grading, there are a number of other effects, which include the following:

(i) grading enables selling by description to take place, providing a basis for the advertising and promotion of standardized products;

(ii) grade standards are essential if futures trading is to take place in a commodity;

(iii) grading is particularly useful if the produce of a number of farms is pooled and marketed collectively;

(iv) grading provides a basis for improved market intelligence;

(v) grading can be used to educate farmers in the improvement of output quality.

Once a grading scheme has been established it should be adhered to rigidly. Changing the standards can lead to a loss of confidence among both producers and consumers, and very soon overcomes the whole object of the scheme. It is advantageous if grades can be clearly marked on the product, and can be easily recognized at all levels of the market. Once grade standards have been set it is vital to ensure that they remain constant. This may entail the employment of inspectors, or else random sampling of output.

There will always be some factors which, while important to consumers, are beyond the scope of any grading scheme. Tenderness and appearance, for example, are important attributes of any meat product, but they are almost impossible to incorporate into a grading scheme. The feasibility of grading varies according to the type of agricultural commodity being considered. There are considerable variations in types of livestock, for example; however, there is little precise knowledge concerning consumer tolerance of different variations in standards.

Even if desirable characteristics are identified it is still difficult for them to be recognized on a carcass and even more so from a live animal. Even if classification does take place at the wholesale level, the grades specified can often be lost before the meat reaches the retail level. Although classification schemes exist in the United Kingdom for beef and lamb, it is almost certain that at present maximum benefit is not obtained from the advantages of grading in livestock production.

Egg production offers a complete contrast. Here the important quality characteristics are size, absence of cracks, and absence of blood spots. These are easy to identify, and grading is widely used to segregate the market into homogeneous groups of different value. The other commodity for which grading is widely used in the United Kingdom is horticultural products. Such products similarly lend themselves to grading, and large scale orders can be placed in advance in terms of specified grades. This increases the efficiency of the marketing operation.

One final point must be considered in relation to grading standards, however. It is important that the standards are based on characteristics which are important to the ordinary consumer rather than on the views of technical experts. In the absence of this, grades specified may fail to gain consumer acceptance. In reality it might be difficult to obtain reliable information on consumer preferences.

Arguments in favour of compulsory grading systems are based very heavily on the assumption that the grades implemented reflect the purchasing patterns of consumers and the trade. In fact this may not be the case. Bowbrick (1979) investigated the quality of strawberries obtained by consumers via a pick-your-own enterprise. From this it was possible to observe what consumers chose to buy when given a free choice. Analysis of the fruit picked showed that only 3 per cent of the samples picked by consumers met EEC standards. There appeared to be very little relationship between grading standards and consumer preferences.

Grading is of greatest importance to the farmer if a marketing contract is entered into, because the level of payment will almost certainly be related to some grading standard. Grading is also of greater importance if export markets are made use of. In the UK as a whole comparatively little use is made of grading, although this does not hold for every country in the world. In the United States, for example, there are statutory grading schemes for meat, grains, and potatoes.

Applicability of market information

It is very difficult to provide a definition of exactly what market information is. It comprises, basically, any information which is relevant to the production or marketing of an agricultural commodity. This information would provide knowledge about the consumption, production, imports, exports, stocks, prices, and so on of the product in question.

It is essential to start from the basis that all participants in agricultural markets are imperfectly informed, and that it is in the interests of agricultural producers that the information which is provided should be improved.

There are three broad classifications of market information:

1. *Short-term information* which is designed to achieve optimum allocation of produce which has already been harvested, or animals which are ready for sale.

2. *Medium-term information* which is relevant for commodities which are in the process of production, but which are not yet ready for sale. This will include information on trends in production costs and prices, and so on.

3. *Long-term information* which gives trends for the coming years, to help in the selection of new enterprises on the farm, or the curtailment of existing enterprises, in order to reduce the speculation risk. This requires completely different information to that for short term decisions.

All farmers undoubtedly have a need for market information, since it can be used as an aid to improving decision making. The dissemination of market intelligence enables the marketing system to function more efficiently by reducing uncertainty. The provision of accurate market information can help the farmer to improve both his production and his marketing decisions. Production decisions will be aided in particular by the provision of accurate medium- and long-term information, and marketing decisions will be improved by the provision of any relevant and accurate information.

The nature of the farmers' requirements with respect to market information will differ, however, according to the type of information. In the short term the information which is required is concerned with buying and selling *intentions*, since it is these which will affect prices. Historic data, such as recent price levels, can only provide background information. Sources of short-term information in the United Kingdom are usually Government agencies, for example the Meat and Livestock Commission and sometimes commercial marketing firms and agencies.

Ideally up-to-date information on the price and quantity of different qualities of products offered through different outlets should be provided. The usefulness of price data is very highly correlated with the extent to which it refers to quality and quantity of production, since prices may vary for a number of reasons. For example, they may vary because of differences in the distance of markets from important centres of consumption, or because of some local market imperfection, such as a local demand for a particular type of animal, or because the quality of the products offered for sale is different.

In contrast, medium-term market information helps the farmer to decide where and when to sell over a longer period of time, suggesting the quality and type of production to be aimed for. Similarly, the purpose of long-term market information is to increase confidence in long-term decision making, and to minimize the risks arising from these long term decisions.

There is a very wide variety of sources of market information available throughout British agriculture. These range from official sources such as Ministry of Agriculture, Fisheries, and Food publications, and information provided by bodies such as the Milk Marketing Board, Meat and Livestock Commission, and the Home Grown Cereals Authority, through semi-official sources such as the press, radio and television, and commercial bank publications, to unofficial sources such as University departmental reports, commercial firms' publications and informal conversations among farmers and trade representatives.

These are just some examples of the market information which is available for farmers; in total, vast quantities are produced. A very important consideration in the provision of information is its accuracy.

It can be reasonably argued that if it is not possible to provide accurate market information then none should be provided at all. Farmers need to make a very large number of decisions in the operation of their business and these decisions can be either helped or hindered by the utilization of market information. If the information is accurate then the decisions will be aided; however, if the information is inaccurate, very serious long-term damage can be done to the prestige of agencies which provide market information.

A very good example of the potential danger of inaccurate market information came in 1973-4 with the suggestion by the British Government of a stable long-term future for beef production in the UK as a result of joining the EEC. This was quickly followed by a glut of cattle rearing, and low prices, which proved financially disastrous for beef farmers. A similar situation was discovered by Chivers and Kirk (1967) in a study of the accuracy of market price intelligence for dessert apples. A comparison was made, over a 4 week period, between Government price information for Cox's orange pippins, and information produced from a 25 per cent sample of producers and marketing organizations. This information was used to work out actual market prices, and it was discovered that the actual price over the time period was 8-9 old pence per lb, although Ministry figures suggested a price of 10 old pence per lb. The range in market prices given by the Ministry also proved to be biased, giving a smaller range than was indicated by the more accurate figures.

These examples illustrate the inaccuracy which exists in the market information which is available to farmers. It is possible that the quality could be improved by encouraging producers to collect their own information, however, cost is probably the major barrier here, when considered in relation to the likely benefits. Having said this, all farmers can succeed to a certain extent without information, by intuitive decision making, and the best, or luckiest, will survive very successfully in this way.

Despite this fact the majority of farmers have a great deal to gain from the provision of accurate market information. However, unless and until sources of information justify a proven reputation for accuracy and reliability then the current heavy dependence on intuitive judgement will continue. If it is accepted that an improvement in standards is a desirable aim, three major possibilities present themselves. These are:

1. Grading, in an endeavour to produce two basic economic effects, firstly improvements in operating efficiency, with production aimed towards the most remunerative grades, and secondly improvements in pricing accuracy.
2. A sense of restraint exercised by agricultural forecasters. A great deal of damage is caused by University departments and Government bodies making price and quantity forecasts which are all too quickly proven wrong.
3. Further research, which needs to be carried out into the trends which underly agricultural markets, in order to be able to better understand the cyclical fluctuations which beset agricultural production and marketing.

The question remains, however, of who should pay for the provision of market information? In the United Kingdom at the present time the bulk of market intelligence is provided free to farmers by official and semi-official advisory bodies.

Overall conclusions

It can be concluded that farmers, in general, utilize marketing techniques; however, this is usually in a much more individual and specific way than in the majority of industries. The potential for application increases in proportion to the size of the enterprise and is particularly appropriate where farmers join together for some part of their business activities. Stated briefly, the overall situation is one where marketing is carried out in agriculture, although not all farmers utilize marketing techniques in the disposal of their output.

The present position is epitomized by the work of Mitchell in his investigation of the use made of published market intelligence by farmers in the south west of England. He found that farmers were influenced in their choices of methods of selling by many factors which are not, and probably cannot, be brought within the scope of published market intelligence. Examples of such factors are the supposed greater convenience of one method, specialist non-farming relationships between some farmers and deadweight centres, lack of trust in deadweight centres, an enjoyment of auction markets for social reasons and a detestation of auction markets for personal reasons.

Of the reasons given by farmers for choosing a particular method of sale, it was judged that 59 per cent dealt with factors which do not fall within the purview of published market intelligence. So although market information has a role to play as a positive aid to market orientation at present it is used only to a limited extent in agriculture, which is almost certainly to the industry's disadvantage.

Part II. Legislation affecting Agricultural marketing

4. The history of government support to agriculture

The origins of government support

All reviews of changes which have taken place over time must choose some starting point, however arbitrary that choice might appear. This review of the development of British domestic government regulation of agriculture begins in 1917, since it was then that the British government took the first positive steps of intervention in the marketing of general commodities. Prior to that time, agriculture had operated under free trading conditions following the repeal of the Corn Laws in 1846. Laissez faire worked reasonably well in the second half of the nineteenth century, with production reaching record levels in the 1870s. Thereafter, however, the spectre of plentiful supplies of imported food created increased competition, particularly cheap grain from the prairies of North America, and refrigerated meat and dairy products from Argentina and Australia.

This increase in competition resulted in lower prices and reduced profit margins for farmers, however, there was no move from the Government to support agriculture, primarily because its political influence declined sharply between 1868 and 1900. In the former year, 44 per cent of the total economic interests held by Members of the House of Commons could be attributed to land, whereas by 1900 the corresponding figure was only 23 per cent. Added to this the economic interests of the nation were running strongly against agriculture, with a two-way trading structure of cheap raw imports including food and finished product exports.

It took 3 years of intense warfare to produce Government action to support agriculture, and even this support was short-lived. The threat to food supplies created by the First World War encouraged the introduction in 1917 of the Corn Production Act. This established a system of guaranteed prices for cereals, along with some controls over acreage planted, in an endeavour to encourage the growths of cereals. At the same time a maximum wage to be paid in agriculture was established, administered by the Central Wages Board along with district committees.

Unfortunately, the price levels set by the Act were fixed too high, and when world wheat prices slumped in 1921 the Act was repealed. Wheat fell from £4.04 per quarter in 1921 to £2.13 the following year and only sympathetic consideration from the banking system prevented wholesale bankruptcy among farmers. The repeal of the Act came suddenly and unexpectedly, leaving agriculture to face the rigours of an intense post war depression.

Inter-war support

Throughout the 1920s the industry received very little support, although a committee of enquiry was instituted under the chairmanship of Linlithgow (1924) with the following terms of reference 'To inquire into methods and costs of selling and distributing agricultural, horticultural, and dairy produce in Great Britain, and to consider whether, and if so, by what means, the disparity between the price received by the producer, and that paid by the consumer can be diminished'. The impetus for the enquiry came from the dissatisfaction of farmers concerning their current returns from the market, and the findings of the committee can be summarized as follows:

1. There was a spread between consumers and producers prices which was unjustifiably high, however, the functions of wholesalers, processors, etc. were necessary.
2. One way of overcoming this problem was to introduce a system of standardizing agricultural produce.
3. In order to minimize the gap between consumer and producer prices, it was essential for farmers to form co-operatives of one type or another.
4. Co-operatives, once formed, might rationalize the whole process of the manufacture of agricultural produce, and regulate supplies.
5. On every ground it was better if re-adjustments were made by the industry itself, rather than by legislative compulsion which had a number of deterrent effects on initiative and development.

As a result of the report findings, farmers were encouraged to set about forming co-operatives, and a number of groups covering various commodities were instituted by farmers in the 1920s. Almost all were unsuccessful, mainly as a result of individuals placing themselves before the interests of the group. Perhaps the best example of the lack of success was English Hopgrowers Ltd set up in 1925 in an attempt to reduce the wide fluctuations of price with supply. This co-operative had perhaps the best chance of succeeding of any at that time, since it related to one single-use crop, grown in a restricted area of the United Kingdom.

Ninety per cent of hop growers joined the co-operative, agreeing to sell collectively to the brewers. In the first year an attractive agreement was reached with the brewers and the co-operative enjoyed success. As a result of increased yields, however, in the following years the supply of hops to the co-operative exceeded their contracts and so a pool price was paid to members, which was lower than the returns being obtained by non-members of the co-operative. This resulted in some members withdrawing from the organization and selling directly to the brewers. Eventually English Hopgrowers Ltd. went into liquidation in 1929. It should be noted that a contributory factor to the failure of the co-operative was the fact that there was freedom of import of any quantity of hops into the country, along with other agricultural commodities, further depressing the market.

A drastic change in public agricultural policy, so far as it affected marketing, came as a result of the great economic depression which started in 1929. From this point began the modern period of state intervention, assistance, and control, although the objectives and the methods were quite different in the early days to those which followed. Agriculture was regarded as one of a group of depressed basic industries along with coal, steel, and cotton textiles. The policy instrument decided upon to improve the state of agriculture was the marketing board, and as a result came the Agricultural Marketing Acts of 1931 and 1933. These were enabling acts, allowing compulsory producer marketing boards to be set up under specified conditions. This was achieved by allowing a number of persons, representative of the producers of a given commodity, to draw up a scheme for a collective marketing organization which would control all the supplies of a given commodity.

Great Britain was not the first nation to introduce marketing boards—Canada and Australia had first set them up in the 1920s. In both cases the institution of boards had followed unsuccessful attempts by farmers to form their own marketing organizations, with the farmers eventually resorting to Governmental assistance. The establishment of a cohesive group was essential for the success of a marketing board, and it was intended that they should not become permanent features of the industry, being attempts to sort out current problems and to encourage greater organization. In reality, it proved that once the Acts were passed they became a permanent feature of the marketing of some agricultural commodities.

As a result of this legislation, producer-elected boards were established for milk, potatoes, and hops, succeeding to a certain extent in stabilizing prices through the regulation of supplies and markets. In addition to the boards, an Agricultural Commission was set up with the aims of introducing subsidies, and controlling and regulating supplies. Throughout the 1930s there was a spate of legislation, with a series of Acts being passed which dealt with particular commodities, attempting to provide some form of price regulation through commodity commissions. In effect, these Commissions were relatively unsuccessful, but they did provide a model for later developments.

In 1931, substantial tariffs were introduced for certain horticultural products. The main instrument which was used for protection against overseas imports was, however, not tariffs but import quotas, imposed by agreement with overseas suppliers upon bacon, ham, mutton, and beef. There were also experimental international agreements for the regulation of supplies of wheat, beef, and sugar. Finally price subsidies were introduced for a wide range of products including sugar beet, wheat, barley, oats, and fat cattle.

The most important was the wheat subsidy which came about as a result of the Wheat Act of 1932, whose aim was to encourage the extension of wheat cultivation by ensuring farmers a secure market, and a reasonable price for good quality wheat produced. This was to be achieved by a deficiency payments scheme, paying the difference between the standard price set by the Ministry of Agriculture for a period, and the average market price realized during that period, and was paid on a sliding scale, varying with total output. The aim was to ensure that farmers produced the quality of goods which consumers require. The finance to run the scheme was raised by a levy on all imported flour, and it was intended that the functions of the Wheat Commission, established to run the scheme, could be taken over by a marketing board, if one was set up for wheat.

A subsidy had been in existence to encourage the production of sugar beet since 1925, and had been introduced for two major reasons. The first was that the technology of producing, processing, and distributing tropical sugar cane had been vastly improved since the First World War. This provided a threat to domestic sugar beet production. Second, the danger of a war-time food blockade was always present, and it was decided that domestic production should be encouraged at the expense of overseas supplies.

The Sugar Industry Reorganisation Act of 1936 continued the subsidies, and reorganized the industry by setting up the British Sugar Corporation, which took over the existing sugar beet processing factories and exercised a monopoly in the production of sugar beet in the UK. It became responsible for contracting with the farmer each year for his beet acreage, for processing the crop, and for selling the raw and refined sugar at prices based on the world price. The industry was supervised by the British Sugar Corporation.

Attempts had been made to set up a Livestock Marketing Board in 1934, 1935, and 1936. These proved to be technically impossible and so in 1937 the Livestock Industry Act established a Livestock Commission. It was given five objectives:

(i)   to assist from public funds the producers of fat cattle, by a deficiency payments scheme;
(ii) to control the import of meat;
(iii) to increase the efficiency of the marketing of livestock;
(iv) to enable and to encourage various sections of the industry to promote service schemes; anything which might improve the production, distribution, and marketing of livestock. This included breed improvement research, data collection and improvements in the grading and standardization of livestock;
(v)   to attempt to improve the slaughtering and processing of livestock.

The last major piece of legislation to be introduced before the Second World War was the 1938 Bacon Industry Act. This set up a

Bacon Development Board which was intended to oversee the whole of the bacon industry. Its major functions were:

(i)   to require the Pigs and Bacon Marketing Boards to act in accordance with its directions;

(ii) to submit for Ministry approval any scheme for the nationalization of the bacon industry;

(iii) to prohibit bacon production on any premises not licensed by the Bacon Development Board. It could also sell premises which were no longer in use, in order to raise funds;

(iv) to undertake education, research, and other programmes at will.

If for any reason the Pigs and Bacon Marketing Boards disappeared, all their functions could be taken over by the Bacon Development Board.

Some of the measures introduced in the 1930s, particularly those relating to marketing boards, have had a lasting influence upon the techniques of agricultural support. At the same time such policy was introduced under circumstances of depression and restriction. In fact, the apparatus of protection proved of little benefit to producers, except in the case of horticulture. Price subsidies were more successful in achieving their aims, although the bulk of support was given to wheat and sugar beet growers, favouring the arable farmers of eastern England. This inhibited the economically desirable shift to livestock farming. Throughout the 1930s there was a small rise in agricultural incomes; however, agriculture as a whole remained in a very depressed condition.

With the outbreak of war in 1939 the whole apparatus of agricultural support was abandoned and the Ministry of Food took over the control of agriculture. Maximized output was the major aim, and marketing measures reflected this objective. Local Representative Committees were set up with a far reaching control over agricultural production. Arable farming was encouraged through the issue of compulsory cropping orders, and large numbers of pigs, poultry, and cattle had to be slaughtered because food-stuffs could not be spared to feed them. Although the whole pattern of farming was drastically changed, it brought with it an increase in agricultural prosperity through the introduction of Government guaranteed prices, supported by food rationing. This mechanism continued as a major plank of agricultural support until long after the end of the Second World War.

Post-second world war policies

In 1945 the great body of informed opinion favoured a system of guaranteed prices for agriculture, related to the costs of production and giving a reasonable return to the farmer. This guarantee would be provided in return for an obligation that land would be farmed in an efficient manner. This implied an acceptance of state control and state guarantees as the best method of disposing of the agricultural output of the country. After a great deal of discussion concerning the best way in which to organize agricultural marketing, the 1947 Agricultural Act was introduced. This proved to form the base of government policy over the next 20 years. The provisions for which the Act was to have effect are embodied in the phrase with which the Act has become synonymous:

> To promote and maintain a stable and efficient agricultural industry, capable of producing such part of the nation's food and other agricultural produce in the United Kingdom as in the national interest it is desirable to produce, and to produce it at minimum prices consistent with proper remunerations and living conditions for farmers and agricultural workers, and an adequate return on capital invested in the industry.

The Act was designed to promote efficiency and stability, and required an annual review of economic conditions and prospects of agriculture, to decide the level of guarantees which should be provided for a stated list of commodities accounting for around 80 per cent of agricultural output. The mechanism by which support was given differed over the years. At first the Ministry of Food continued its controls, encouraging maximum output and providing guaranteed prices. This continued until 1951 when the Ministry of Food was abolished, with agricultural support provided through a system of deficiency payments whereby the producer sold in the open market, then the average price of all sales was taken and the Government paid the difference between this average price and a guaranteed price.

The system can be explained as follows. In a given marketing period a guaranteed price would be set for a commodity such as barley of, for example, £g per ton. A farmer selling barley in that period might receive £x per ton, where x could be more, or less, than g, depending on marketing conditions. The sales of all farmers during the marketing period are taken into account to produce an average price, say £a per ton. All farmers who sold barley in that marketing period are then paid a subsidy of £$(g-a)$ per ton. As a result the farmer receives a total price for his barley of £$x + (g-a)$ per ton. If a is greater than g then no subsidy is paid. The advantage of the system was that since each farmer received the average payment, there was an incentive for him to sell at the highest price. However, in practice there were also disadvantages. A measure which was designed to encourage maximum output quickly became a recipe for overproduction.

Another effect of the abolition of the Ministry of Food was that marketing boards were free to be reintroduced, if this were the wish of the producers. The conditions were the same as those provided for in the 1931 and 1933 Agricultural Marketing Acts, although there was a slight modification as a result of the 1949 Agricultural Marketing Act. The main purpose of this Act was to ensure that producer marketing boards, if and when established or revived, should be made amenable to public supervision. To achieve this the Minister of Agriculture was given the power to appoint up to one fifth of the members of each board. In addition any use by a Board of its regulatory powers could be overruled in certain circumstances by the Minister of Agriculture.

The other dominant feature of 1947, aside from the Agriculture Act, so far as the marketing of agricultural products was concerned, was the presentation of the Lucas Committee report on agricultural marketing. The Lucas Committee had been appointed by the immediate post war Labour Government to examine the continuing place of marketing schemes in agriculture. The conclusion of the Committee was that price guarantees provided the farmer with adequate economic protection, and as a result there was no justification for compulsory marketing monopolies. It was felt that the future value of producer-elected boards would be in their ability to improve the presentation and quality of farm produce and to deal with marketing, up to, but no further than, the point of first purchase. Boards were not considered to be suitable mechanisms for the control of distribution beyond this point.

The alternative method of marketing agricultural produce, suggested in the Lucas Report, was the use of Government appointed Commissions, which would be given all the regulatory and trading powers previously available to marketing boards, and it was anticipated that these would be more successful in improving the distribution system. These general conclusions were reinforced by the report, in the same year, of the Williams Committee on milk distribution. This report found producers' boards to be unsuitable agents for improving the efficiency of milk marketing, and produced specific evidence in favour of the creation of an independent marketing commission.

The Lucas report met widespread criticism from within the agricultural industry. Marketing boards had become regarded as a safe option by both farmers and the Government, bringing a measure of stability to markets which had previously been prone to instability, and in particular the National Farmers Union was opposed to what became known as 'Lucas logic'. This may have been partly prompted by the fact that the Union had acquired a dominant measure of control of the pre-war producer boards, and this was an influence which it was not prepared to lose without a fight. After prolonged discussions the Lucas Report was referred for further study, and the 1949 Agricultural Marketing Act was introduced.

A 4 year production plan for agriculture was introduced in 1947, with a planned expansion of net agricultural output of 20 per cent. As an incentive towards this, farmers were given increased levels of guaranteed prices. This expansion was fulfilled, by and large, and occurred at the same time as food supplies became more available from other countries throughout the world. By the mid 1950s agriculture had reached something of a crisis, with farmers dependent on subsidies to retain a reasonable standard of living, and with the Government unhappy about the role of those same subsidies in fostering domestic overproduction, at a time when plentiful supplies of cheap imported food were again becoming available. The constantly recurring production versus marketing support arguments were raised once again, with considerable support for the notion that expenditure would be more profitably repaid by supporting the marketing of agricultural output, rather than in subsidizing production.

The plain fact was that the British farmer was faced with the position of having to compete in a market with much cheaper imported products. Because of this some form of direct subsidization was inevitable. In 1954 a new, and extremely complex system of guarantees was introduced. Output was to be sold in the open market at the best price which could be obtained, to which would be added a retrospective subsidy payment, calculated as previously explained. The guarantees for milk, potatoes, and (after 1957) eggs were to be implemented through the agency of producer marketing boards, which would receive sufficient Government subsidy to honour the prices received at annual reviews.

It had long been the practice that the level of agricultural prices was discussed annually by the Minister of Agriculture and representatives of the farming industry, and a review made of the prices to be operative for the ensuing year. The system continues in an amended form through to the present day. For the products which were backed by marketing boards the Government reduced the extent of its commitments. For eggs and potatoes, 'minimum' or 'floor' prices were introduced, which were to operate only when the market was depressed. In practice the 'minimum' price for eggs, although at a slightly lower level than previous guarantees, proved to be consistently well above market prices. For milk, a guaranteed price continued to operate on the old basis, although it was limited to a specified quantity of output. This was the first time that the Government had exercised any control over the physical quantity of production.

The next major piece of legislation to be introduced was the 1957 Agriculture Act. This was related to the opposition of farmers to any reductions in the levels of subsidies. The Government undertook not to reduce the total value of price guarantees by more than 2.5 per cent in any one year, after allowing in full for any change in costs. Individual commodities were protected by the assurance that the value of its guarantee could not be reduced by more than 4 per cent in any one year, or in the case of livestock products by more than 9 per cent over a 3 year period. These measures removed the possibility of sudden large price cuts, particularly in relation to individual commodities.

Changes of emphasis in the 1960s

Throughout the 1960s there were annual reductions in the levels of subsidy payments for nearly all commodities. In addition, the Standard Quantity System was extended in 1963. This had been introduced initially for milk, laying down a stated quantity of output for which the guaranteed price would be paid. Any production in excess of the standard quantity was to be allowed to find its own market level. In order for this measure to succeed, it was essential that overseas imports were effectively controlled, because if the market price of the standard quantity was forced down by a glut of importation then, as a result, the subsidy cost to the Government would again increase.

It can be fairly said that at this time the market support system was inefficient. For certain commodities the deficiency payments system was very complex, creating little confidence for farmers to invest deeply in their production. Throughout the 1960s various modifications were made to the system of supporting product prices through deficiency payments. The general trend was to adopt measures which would be more compatible to Common Market agricultural policy, should membership of that body ever become a reality. In 1962, buffer import prices were introduced for cereals, and a market sharing arrangement devised for bacon in an endeavour to control the pressure of imports on the home market.

Arrangements were also introduced to achieve a more orderly marketing of eggs. The supply of milk, potatoes, and sugar beet had already been regulated for many years by such means as standard quantities and farm acreage quotas. The net effect of the new control measure was to introduce an element of protection into agricultural production which had not existed since the repeal of the Corn Laws. This reached a peak in 1971 with the replacement of deficiency payments by variable import levies on certain commodities. This was a major change in Government policy and reflected the type of movement which would have to be made as part of the Government's intent to enter into an enlarged European Economic Community. The objective of the new scheme was to produce a situation whereby farmers would increasingly secure their returns from the market, and as a result be less dependent on Government support.

With effect from July 1971, the Government introduced interim levy schemes in respect of cereals, beef and veal, mutton and lamb, and some dairy products, but not butter and cheese. The aim was to maintain domestic market prices, by preventing the damage caused by low priced imports. The arrangements were based on minimum import prices supported by levies; if imports were offered for sale below the minimum price, then a levy, equal to the difference between the minimum and the lowest offer prices was to be applied on all imports of that commodity.

Initially the levy scheme operated alongside a modified defiency payments scheme, and developments continued, particularly after 1 January 1973 when British dreams of European espousement became a reality, and the United Kingdom became a member of the European Economic Community. Farmers were introduced to the discipline of Common Agricultural Policy, and market support systems were adapted correspondingly. The practicalities of such a change are the province of the next chapter. However, before moving on to European legislation there is one other aspect of domestic agricultural policy which is worthy of consideration in so far as it affects the marketing of agricultural commodities.

It became clear from the 1950s onwards that, as a result of changing conditions, an entirely different approach could be adopted in agricultural policy. A revolution was taking place in the marketing of food at the retail level, bringing with it a requirement for production to meet uniform standards in order to improve returns. In addition agricultural technology was changing, with increasing sizes of units allowing large scale contracts. Intensive systems of production were also becoming more commonplace, allowing changes in retail patterns to occur more quickly.

The re-introduction of commodity commissions

This induced the Government to rethink its approach to the marketing of agricultural commodities, with commissions once again viewed as a desirable means of improving the efficiency of, not only immediate production and distribution, but also other aspects of farm production, such as changing the style of production to meet the demands of consumers. As a result two pieces of legislation were introduced, the 1965 Cereals Marketing Act forming the Home Grown Cereals Authority and the 1967 Agriculture Act creating, among other things, the Meat and Livestock Commission. These Commissions have played an important part in the improvement of agricultural marketing in the United Kingdom since their inception and in concluding this chapter a review will be made of their development over time, and the way in which they work.

1. *Home Grown Cereals Authority*

In the early 1960s market prices for home-grown grain were depressed by the pressure of high supplies—home and foreign—and with no regulations on imports, it was difficult to improve the phasing and marketing of home supplies. Total deficiency payments for cereals were rising, and in 1963/64 they reached £77m.

In 1964 the Government decided to introduce minimum import price arrangements for cereals, combined with the concept of standard quantities for home-grown wheat and barley. In the same year discussions were held between the Government and representatives of producers, merchants and processors on possible ways of giving effect to the broad objective of improved marketing of home-grown cereals.

It was generally agreed that home-grown grain could compete more effectively with imported grain if supplies came forward throughout the year to match the demands of the market, if users had a greater assurance of continuity of supply, and if more comprehensive market information was available. It was also agreed that, to secure these improvements, a marketing organization representative of the main cereal interests, and with independent members, should be set up with appropriate statutory powers.

In June 1965 the Cereals Marketing Act created as a statutory body the Home-Grown Cereals Authority. Its basic purpose is to improve the marketing of home-grown cereals—wheat, barley, oats, and rye. In 1970 maize was added for a limited number of non-trading functions. Its main functions are to encourage the more orderly marketing of cereals throughout the season and to provide improved market intelligence. The Authority comprises 23 members, appointed by the Minister of Agriculture. Five have no direct connection with the industry, with the Chairman and Deputy Chairman appointed by the Minister from these independent members, nine are farmers feeding some home-grown cereals to their livestock, and nine merchants or users of cereals such as compounders, millers, and maltsters. The Authority regards its main purpose of improving the marketing of home-grown cereals as:

(i) stimulating the maximum possible use of UK grains; encouraging efficient marketing methods to ensure timely supplies of the right type and quality to meet spot and forward demands as they arise; and helping to achieve fair and reasonable market prices; (ii) influencing policy and procedural developments to help achieve (i) within the framework laid down by the UK government and EEC regulations.

The work of the Home Grown Cereals Authority can be divided into five major areas.

1. *The provision of market intelligence*
The authority publishes a weekly bulletin of price information. It contains such information as:
(i)   prices of a variety of grains locally and nationally;
(ii) prices of grains competing (EEC and world) at major UK ports for up to 4 months ahead;
(iii) tonnage of recorded sales;
(iv) London grain futures prices;
(v)   prices of grain at important continental centres;
(vi) licences, and tonnages, to import grain from third countries.

2. *Undertaking economic and marketing research*
At its inception the Authority lacked up-to-date information on the whole complex of the UK cereals market. No survey of the UK market had taken place since 1928. One of the Authority's first actions was to commission Professor D.K. Britton to undertake an independent and comprehensive survey of the whole market. The Britton Report of some 800 pages was published in February 1969 (Britton 1969). Since then a number of surveys and reports have followed, including Information in the cereals market, agricultural marketing and the EEC, and the impact of the EEC on UK cereals marketing. The economic research work is guided by a panel appointed by the Authority.

3. *Scientific research and development*
The Authority does not itself carry out research, but promotes research by grants to existing institutions. It places emphasis on means of increasing the use of domestic cereals rather than on production aspects, except in so far as suitability for a particular market or demand is influenced by factors arising at the production stage; this in essence being the first stage of the whole marketing process.

4. Contract bonus scheme

The object of the scheme was to encourage growers to make forward contracts for the delivery of grain at least 2 months in advance. Growers registered forward contracts with the Authority, and on their due fulfilment were paid bonuses.

The first scheme covered the 1965/1966 cereals year and up to 1972/73 there were eight schemes. Registrations for barley and wheat together amounted to up to 4 million tons per year. Since then no schemes have been proposed, the official explanation being that since growers and buyers have become familiar with techniques of forward trading a high level of forward contracting would continue because of commercial considerations. Powers still remain within the Act to allow bonus schemes to be reintroduced.

5. Other powers available to the authority

(a) Bonus on delivery schemes—similar to Cereals Deficiency Payments Scheme.
(b) Bonus and guarantees on forward contracts (to growers).
(c) Support buying, storage and disposal—intervention buying can now operate as part of the EEC systems of support. The Authority acts as executive agent for the Intervention Board for Agricultural Produce, carrying out buying, storage and disposal functions for cereals and oilseed rape.
(d) Denaturing of wheat: the Authority administers the control arrangements for denaturing: the EEC market support system designed to avoid a surplus of wheat on the flour milling market by subsidising its use for animal feeding.

The expenditure of the Home-Grown Cereals Authority falls under the two main headings of administration and research. The cost is financed equally from two main sources, an Exchequer contribution and a levy on cereal growers. Intervention agency work is financed by the Intervention Board and the Agriculture Departments.

The Authority has established a central position in the cereals marketing complex. Because of this it exercises a considerable influence on the determination of policy, national and otherwise, affecting the cereals market. The main part of the Authority's work is concerned with guiding cereals marketing practices to keep abreast of, and anticipate, any changes which are taking place. The Authority, therefore, while not playing a direct part in the marketing of cereals, has an important indirect influence on the operation of the market.

2. *The Meat and Livestock Commission*

The 1967 Agriculture Act established the Meat and Livestock Commission, chiefly as a result of the recommendations of the Verdon Smith Report (1964). This was a combination of the already existing Pig Industry Development Authority (PIDA), the Beef Recording Association, and the Ministry of Agriculture Fat-stock service. In the Act the Commission was given the general duty of:

> promoting greater efficiency in the livestock industry and the livestock products industry, and in carrying out their functions the Commission should have due regard to the interests of consumers as well as to the interests of the various sections of the livestock industry and the livestock products industry.

Three main sectors were specified where efficiency was to be improved: production, marketing, and distribution.

When the Meat and Livestock Commission (MLC) was set up, the meat trade was violently opposed to its inception. Meat retailers declared a policy of non-co-operation, and there was also strong opposition from the wholesale industry. This has now completely changed and the image of MLC is much improved.

To finance the cost of running the MLC, a levy is raised from the livestock industry, which is imposed at the point of slaughter. This does not apply to imported meat and animals exported live. The levy has increased considerably with time as the work of the Commission has expanded. In 1979 it stood at 90p per head for beef cattle, 16p per head for sheep, 30p per head for pigs, and 8p per head for calves.

This provides about half of MLC's income. Additional remuneration comes from Government agency work, and Government classification work. The MLC employs a full time staff of between 1200 and 1300, plus 120 livestock field staff, and 180 involved with fatstock certification work. Also the commission runs five pig testing stations and five bull testing stations.

In 1967 three advisory committees were set up. These were
(a) the Production Committee;
(b) the Distribution Committee;
(c) the Consumer Committee.

Their role was to advise the Commission on any parts of the livestock industry which fell within their sphere of influence.

The Commission itself, was to consist of not more than ten members appointed by the Minister of Agriculture through qualifications of financial, commercial, technical, scientific, administrative, or other relevant experience, without financial or commercial interest which would prejudice the proper discharge of their functions as members.

The Production and Distribution Committees have now been abolished, and direct consultation between members of the Commission and the various sections of the industry is very much encouraged. The Consumers Committee has been retained since it was felt that this was the most effective method of taking note of consumer interests.

The major function of the Meat and Livestock Commission is probably livestock improvement, covering cattle, sheep, and pigs. There are two areas where it has attempted to upgrade performance, through the genetic selection of improved animals, and through improved systems of production. PIDA had established pig improvement schemes—mainly feed and litter recording. This was reversed after the MLC was set up and it was decided to continue central testing, and to introduce nucleus reserve herds and nucleus multiplying units. Litter recording was discontinued.

MLC has been charged with the administration and development of carcass classification schemes for livestock—this is a language of communication to describe the attributes of carcasses. It is applicable to retailers and producers, and the aim is to improve market information. Classification attempts to simplify and to improve the efficiency of livestock marketing by providing a descriptive code for use by the whole industry. It does not grade, however, but allows a simple and quick identification of carcass attributes to be made. Initially there was widespread opposition to the scheme, and although it has won gradual acceptance, the problem of who has to bear the cost of classification still remains.

There is also a slaughterhouse advisory service. Each year about 160-170 projects are handled by the Department. Until recently this was a free service. Market development work is also carried out. This is a mixed bag of services, putting out a large number of publications; however, there is still room for improvement in the take up of Commission development work.

In its early years MLC had a very small publicity and promotion budget, for example £115 000 in 1973-74; however, in the mid 1970s this changed, mainly at the behest of the NFU. The result was the setting up of the Meat Promotion Executive, which has the task of promoting sales of British meat through television advertising, consumer education, home economics, and so on.

The budget of the Meat Promotion Executive, which is raised from part of the levy on animals at the point of slaughter, is considerable; in 1977 it was in excess of £2 million. In 1979 the amounts allotted to the Meat Promotion Executive were 30p per head for cattle, 8½p per head for sheep, 15p per head for pigs, and 3p per head for calves.

The MLC makes various contributions to meat marketing research, partly sponsoring the work of the Meat Research Institute. In addition a sum of money is usually allotted each year to be spent on post-graduate scholarship and fellowship schemes, and grants to university departments for research.

Market information provision is a very important part of the work of the MLC. Two quarterly publications are issued, being mainly situation and outlook reports. They give forecasts of numbers, prices, etc. There is a conscious policy to encourage the public media to carry as much MLC information as possible.

A major complaint concerning the provision of market information has been that by the time it is published the information is out of date. To overcome this a rapid information service has been instituted, giving same-day price information from a sample of 138 auction centres in the UK. A more detailed and less speedy sample is also drawn of 64 UK markets for the Government. This is used to calculate the UK cattle reference price which goes to Brussels. MLC also run EEC telex services, giving a variety of forecasts.

MLC are also active in the field of forecasting, giving short-term and longer-term information. An EEC liaison officer works in the MLC Economics Department, and much of the information collected is published in Brussels.

The most important future work of the Commission probably lies in two major areas.

(i) There is widespread disagreement with the principles of carcass classification at the levels of both trade and production. Until the schemes are accepted by farmers and butchers alike then the system will work neither efficiently, nor effectively.

(ii) The majority of farmers do not avail themselves of the wealth of information which is available at present. There is still wide-scale ignorance of the work and potentialities of MLC.

Like the Home-Grown Cereals Authority, the Meat and Live-stock Commission can claim a certain degree of success since its inception. Both bodies suffer from a lack of 'bite' to enable them to reinforce their policies; however, they have at the same time contributed to an improvement in the efficiency of the marketing of their respective commodities, to an extent which is unlikely to have been surpassed by the alternative of producer marketing boards.

5. European Agricultural Policy: its relevance to farmers

The origins of the Community

On 25 March 1957 the governments of France, West Germany, Italy, the Netherlands, Belgium, and Luxemburg signed the Treaty of Rome. In so doing they created what is now known as the European Economic Community (EEC), or less accurately, the Common Market. Upon its foundation the aim of the Community was to bring into being a vast single market for all goods, which would constitute a powerful productive unit and generate steady expansion, greater stability, and a more rapid rise in living standards.

Initially Great Britain stood outside the Community and, as a result, the British farmer was initially relatively unaffected by the decision that the Common Market should extend to agriculture and trade in agricultural products. However, by 1961 Britain had applied for membership and a period of lengthy negotiations began, but it was eventually halted abruptly by the veto of France, in the person of General de Gaulle. A second application followed in 1967 but this was again vetoed by General de Gaulle on the grounds that full membership for Britain would lead to the destruction of the Community. This application stood on the table until after the resignation of General de Gaulle as President of France in 1969. Thereafter, following lengthy negotiations, Great Britain was eventually accepted as a full member of the Community, along with the Republic of Ireland and Denmark.

On 1 January 1973 the United Kingdom became part of the EEC and embarked on a period of transition from independent trading policy to common European policy. Since agriculture was included in the Community, British farmers were greatly affected by the change, particularly in respect to their marketing, because the systems of market support differed greatly between the United Kingdom and Europe.

European agricultural support is administered under the title Common Agricultural Policy (or CAP) and the way in which it has developed is closely related to the backgrounds of the six countries which originally signed the Treaty of Rome. For West Germany the prospect of free trade in industrial goods, and free access to the French market in particular, was extremely inviting. Conversely, France had a relatively efficient agricultural sector, particularly arable production and stood to make substantial inroads into the West German market. It was decided that prices of agricultural products should be uniform throughout the Community. To decide the common price levels, a centralized system was established and also machinery was designed to manipulate markets in order to bring about common prices. A Community system for financing the support policy was also called for.

Another important reason for including agriculture within the Treaty of Rome is the sheer size of the agricultural sector in Europe. In 1958 farming employed fifteen million people, about 20 per cent of the working population of the Community. It was also an industry in which the problem of low incomes was particularly acute and in terms of political horsetrading the European agricultural vote was, and is, so important that agriculture could hardly be ignored.

The aims of CAP are to:

(a) increase agricultural productivity;
(b) ensure a fair standard of living for the agricultural community;
(c) stabilize agricultural methods;
(d) guarantee regular supplies of food; and
(e) ensure reasonable prices to consumers.

Common Agricultural Policy comprises two major elements, a structural policy and a market policy. The structural element is mainly concerned with the number and size of farms and related businesses with, to date, its implementation being left mainly to individual member states, supplemented to a small extent by Community funds. The basic principle of the market element is to allow farm goods to move freely within the Common Market whilst maintaining reasonable farm prices and incomes. It is this principle which has produced the problems and complexities besetting CAP.

The cost of maintaining agricultural policy is raised from the European Agricultural Guidance and Guarantee Fund, commonly known as FEOGA—the initial letters of the official French title: Fonds Europeen d'Orientation et Garantie Agricoles. The organization of FEOGA has been affected by its division into two types of support. The Guidance Section was set up to provide finance for structural improvements and the Guarantee Section was established to be used in relation to market support. The market support element is at present dominant, with the Guidance Section accounting for only about 10 per cent of the expenditure of FEOGA, although it is the overall policy of CAP to transfer an increasing proportion of support to the Guidance Section. This, however, will almost certainly be a long-term consideration.

In 1962-3, when the Community established Common agricultural support systems, whatever sums were required for Fund payments were contributed in certain proportions by the member states. Up to 1965 the proportions were progressively changed with a diminishing part of each member country's liability being determined by the budgetary scale and a rising proportion provided in relation to each country's net imports of agricultural products from non-member states. Over time the methods of financing the Fund have changed. From 1967 to 69, 90 per cent of all levies and customs duties on imports of foodstuffs was handed over by the member country governments to the fund, raising about half of the necessary finance. The remainder was raised by proportional payments by member countries. The present situation is that the Community acquires income from various sources including the levies charged on agricultural imports from non-member countries and the tariff revenues from the Common Customs Tariff. This income is appropriated in the general budget for use in all the activities of the Community requiring finance, including the Common Agricultural Policy.

Market support systems for agricultural commodities

There is a common support system for agricultural commodities, although the machinery differs from commodity to commodity. The income support to farmers is guaranteed by manipulating the market so as to bring about a high enough price to provide adequate remuneration for them. The internal price level is partly maintained by a variety of protective devices at the common frontier. These prevent low-price imports from eroding the internal price level, a situation which existed in the early days of the Community. In addition provision is made for official support buying within the

Community, removing from the market the excess of supply over demand at the predetermined support price level.

This policy was a follow up to the policies pursued at national levels before the signing of the Treaty of Rome; however, it is the opposite of the market support systems which had been utilized in the United Kingdom. As a result the British farmer and the trade had to adapt to a completely different system of market price determination.

Market support arrangements have been continuously developed and expanded to include a wider range of agricultural products. The principle underlying all the regulations is the provision of free movement of products within the Community. The common organization of markets is essentially based on a system of inter-related prices. The official prices framework is fixed each year by the Council of Ministers for the main agricultural products except, at present, mutton and lamb, potatoes, and wool. Target, guide or basic prices are determined, the price which it is hoped producers will realize for their produce in the wholesale markets during the marketing period for which they are fixed.

Intervention prices are then fixed at levels which vary according to the product in question, but below their corresponding target, guide or basic price levels. At this price intervention agencies will buy in all Community produced commodities offered to them. From the basic intervention price of a product, set in a given marketing area, derived intervention prices are determined throughout the community to allow for differences in demand and supply.

Threshold prices are the minimum prices fixed for imports of products into the Community from third countries. This is necessary because in general EEC prices are higher than world prices and thus the Community requires protection from cheap imports from non-EEC countries. To achieve this variable levies are applied to consignments offered at less than the threshold price level, varying as the minimum price of imports varies.

Reference or sluice gate prices are the minimum prices at which products from third countries come into the Community. These are set at levels representing the cost of production in non-member countries and adding on levies to bring these levels up to EEC basic price levels. To allow the EEC to export surplus agricultural products to third countries, export refunds may be granted to allow commodities produced in the Community to be sold to non-member countries at lower world prices, thereby placing Community products in a competitive position to seek outlets in third countries. However, if world prices are higher than Community prices producers are discouraged from selling their produce outside the Common Market by a variable levy placed on exports.

To illustrate the operation of the various prices in practice the market support arrangements for the most important agricultural commodities will be considered now, in turn.

1. *Cereals*

This was the first product to come under the control of CAP, with the common organization distinguishing between two types of cereal, that used for animal feeds and that used for bread making. The aim is to promote a balance between these two types of production, at the same time ensuring an improvement in farm incomes.

A single common intervention price is fixed annually for wheat, barley, and maize. Other intervention prices are fixed for both rye and durum wheat. All intervention prices apply to the Ormes Intervention Centre in France, which is the centre of the Community area having the greatest surplus for all cereals at the wholesale stage. At these price levels the EEC authorities are obliged to buy in all home-grown cereals offered to them. To increase the profitability of wheat of medium bread making quality and to encourage its production in the EEC, a reference price for common wheat of bread making quality is calculated. This reference price is arrived at by adding an amount which reflects the difference in return between the production of common wheat of bread making quality and non-bread making quality to the single common intervention price. Intervention purchases of bread making quality wheat at this reference price are not automatic, with prices only supported at this level if the situation is deemed to warrant it.

Based on the intervention prices, target prices are set for common wheat, durum wheat, and rye and a single common target price for barley and maize, based on Duisburg in West Germany which is the centre of the Community area having the greatest deficit for all cereals at the wholesale stage. The target prices are arrived at by adding the cost of transport between Ormes and Duisburg, plus a market element, to the reference price for common wheat, the single intervention price for rye and durum wheat, and the single common intervention price for barley and maize. The target prices reflect the desired level of market prices for cereals in the future, so far as the EEC authorities are concerned.

To control import prices, an element representing the costs of transporting cereals from Rotterdam to Duisburg is subtracted from the target prices to determine the individual threshold prices for common wheat, durum wheat, and rye and the single common threshold price for barley and maize.

When imports are offered for less than the threshold prices, variable levies, equal for each product to the differences between the threshold prices and the import offer prices, are charged, the levies varying from day to day as the relationships between the import price levels and the threshold prices change. The result should be that selling prices for imported cereals on the Duisburg market should be never less than the target prices.

For exports from the EEC to non-EEC countries, the difference between Community price levels and the world cereals market price levels may be covered by export refunds. All cereal prices are broken down into monthly prices so as to encourage orderly marketing throughout the year as a result of storing cereals.

2. *Milk and milk products*

The aim of the market support measures for milk and milk products is to secure product prices which will enable producers to be paid a target price for milk of 3.7 per cent butter fat. The common target price for milk is fixed annually at the level that it is felt producers should realize for their milk delivered to a dairy. At the consumer or retail stage the price for liquid milk is allowed to find its own level, although, under existing regulations, member states may, at their discretion, fix retail prices for milk for liquid consumption.

The liquid-milk market in the EEC uses only about 20 per cent of the total milk produced, therefore, the maintenance of the target price is achieved by providing intervention prices for butter, skim milk, and some Italian cheese. The prices are set at a level to ensure payment of the liquid-milk target price by allowing for the costs of producing butter, skim milk, or Italian cheese. Imports of milk products are controlled through threshold prices and levies. The Council fix threshold prices with reference to the milk target price, therefore the market selling price of imported products corresponds to the costs of making and selling milk products within the

EEC. Restitution payments on exports of milk and milk products may be granted to cover all or part of the difference between world and EEC prices. In principle trade in liquid milk within the Common Market is possible, however, differing health regulations still provide a hindrance.

Dairying has been one of the major problems facing CAP. A large proportion of small farmers in the Community depend on milk sales for their livelihoods, consequently relatively high target prices have been set for milk to keep this politically important group of farmers in business. The result, however, has been that the EEC is now more than self-sufficient in milk products, the ensuing butter 'mountains' and skim milk 'mountains' being sold from time to time to countries such as Russia, making use of export restitutions.

One of the major causes of the imbalance in dairy production in the EEC is the differing levels of consumption of milk and milk products in the EEC member countries. In the UK consumption is very high, much higher than in any other EEC country; for example in 1977/78 the average consumption of liquid milk was 2.66 litres per week per head of the population. The result is that, although the EEC as a whole is more than self-sufficient for all milk products (resulting in the 'mountains'), the relative self-sufficiency differs between countries. This is illustrated in Table 5.1

Table 5.1. Self-sufficiency ratios of EEC countries
for various milk products in 1978

Country	Butter and butter oil	Cheese	Skimmed and butter milk powder
EEC	117	105	106
Denmark	269	339	156
Eire	350	714	669
Netherlands	528	222	51
UK	40	66	131

Source: MMB (1979).

In an attempt to reduce the extent of overproduction the European Commission have introduced, over time, a number of wide ranging measures. These have included the compulsory incorporation of skim milk powder in animal feeding-stuffs in place of other animal feed proteins in an attempt to get rid of 400 000 tonnes of skim milk powder. The scheme worked reasonably well, but was subsequently held to have been a violation of the basic objectives and rules of the EEC. Another scheme encouraged small-scale milk producers to retire or switch to beef production by financial inducements, popularly known as the 'golden handshake'.

Since September 1977 a co-responsibility levy has been charged on milk delivered to dairies. This is a tax on milk production, in 1977-78 amounting to 1.5 per cent of the target price for milk and raising, in the United Kingdom, £11 million. In principle, funds raised from the levy are available for new projects of an advertising and promotional research nature. It seems likely that, in the future, the co-responsibility levy will be a major plank of Community control of milk production.

3. *Poultry meat and eggs*

Community measures in the UK are mainly concerned with imports. The market within the EEC is free, with no minimum prices or intervention measures, the only regulation being on the quality of eggs. Measures to control imports have been formulated in relation to the Common Market cereals regulations. Poultry producers use large amounts of feed grain sold to them at Community prices, which are in general in excess of world grain prices. This puts producers at a competitive disadvantage. Therefore, by taking into account the world price for feed grains and other costs of production, every quarter the Commission fixes in advance a sluice-gate price which roughly equals what it believes to be the cost of producing the commodity in question outside the EEC. If imports are offered at less than the sluice-gate price, then a supplementary levy is charged to raise the import price to that price. A further basic levy is payable on imports to make allowance for the higher EEC feed costs. This levy is calculated to equalize the difference between feed grain prices on the EEC and world markets. To protect and give preference to EEC producers an additional levy of 7 per cent of the average-sluice gate price in the previous year ending 1 May, is added. The various elements are portrayed in Fig. 5.1.

For exports of poultry meat and eggs export refund payments may be granted at the discretion of the EEC Commission, to offset the difference between EEC and world market prices.

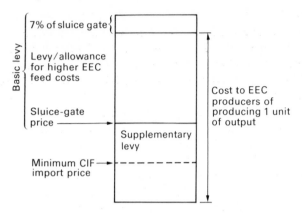

Fig. 5.1. Market support for eggs and poultry meat in the EEC.

4. *Pig meat*

The regulations here are similar to those for poultry meat and eggs. In addition to import controls through sluice-gate prices and levies, however, there are also provisions to support the internal pig meat market. Market intervention measures are not automatically applied at an agreed price, but may be applied if the conditions warrant it at a price between 85 and 92 per cent of the basic price.

Each year the Council fixes the basic price for slaughtered pigs of a standard quality. The basic price is fixed at a level which contributes towards stabilizing market prices without leading to excessive production and stocks of pig meat. If the market price recorded on a selection of representative markets throughout the Community falls below and is likely to remain below 103 per cent of the basic price, intervention buying measures may be taken.

Imports of pig meat are controlled by fixing a sluice-gate price every quarter and applying variable levies to raise the import prices to Community levels. The sluice-gate prices, as for eggs and poultry meat, represent forecasts of the costs of producing pig meat in non-EEC countries. To enable pig meat to be exported to non-EEC countries export refunds may be granted; however, the actual amounts are subject to considerable flexibility under the control of the Commission and the Pig meat Management Committee.

5. Beef and veal

The EEC arrangements for beef and veal are exceedingly complicated. This is because of the long-term problem of poor returns to beef and veal producers, overproduction of the commodities and intra-EEC trade providing certain producers and wholesalers with unacceptable profits.

The common organization of the beef and veal market is based on fixing an annual guide price for live adult cattle and calves; this is the average price which should be realized for the whole year for animals sold for slaughter. Each week reference prices (average wholesale market prices) are calculated for each member state, and for the EEC as a whole. The relationship between reference prices and guide prices determines whether any official market support is necessary.

Intervention facilities are provided for beef and veal, and the intervention price is currently fixed at 90 per cent of the guide price. Basic import levies are also calculated weekly on the basis of the difference between the guide price and the prices at the Community frontier at which imports are offered.

In 1974 there was overproduction of beef and veal and in July the Commission banned imports of beef and veal, except for the quota allowed under GATT and special quotas for some African states. In November the UK rejected intervention measures as failing to adequately support beef producers' incomes and introduced instead a variable premium system. This was accepted by the EEC in February 1975 and at the same time the Commission dropped the intervention price from 93 to 90.43 per cent of the guide price.

In January 1976 a jumelage system was introduced whereby traders were allowed to obtain a licence to import meat for manufacture only after buying meat from the intervention stores. This system was replaced in April 1977 by a new EEC beef-import regime, under which the levy applied to imports is increased to 105, 110 and 114 per cent of its full rate as the reference price falls below 98, 96, and 90 per cent, respectively, of the guide price.

In 1976/77 the variable premium system was continued in the UK, but at a reduced level. As from September 1976, 25 per cent of the cost of the premium was met by FEOGA. Member States may now choose one of two alternative methods of granting aid to cattle producers. The method preferred in the UK is to pay a variable premium for the slaughter of adult cattle, other than cows, which have originated within the EEC. Over a year, the value of the premium plus the average price realized for fat cattle sold must not exceed 85 per cent of the guide price, or 88 per cent of the guide price at any specific point in time.

In the UK a variable premium is paid to producers selling fat cattle in any week when the average UK market price for certified cattle has been less than the target price for the week in question. The target price is set annually in the UK at no more than 85 per cent of the EEC guide price, and weekly target prices are calculated to encourage orderly marketing throughout the year.

The alternative method of support which can be used is to pay a fixed premium for each calf born and which is proved to be still alive 6 months after birth.

In October 1977 the Commission suggested to the Council of Ministers a number of changes to the beef and veal market support arrangements. These were put forward because the current measures were attempting to maintain beef prices at too high a level in comparison to prices for pig meat and poultry meat. The proposals included measures to allow for both weak and strong market situations. A strong market situation occurs when market prices are above 98 per cent of the guide prices, and a weak market situation occurs when the market prices are below 98 per cent of the guide prices.

If the reference price was to rise above 98 per cent of the guide price then the levy charged on imports would be automatically reduced. Also the Commission could introduce slaughter premia on dairy cows and heifers to increase the supply of beef and reduce prices.

With reference prices below 98 per cent import levies would be increased, if they fell below 93 per cent the Commission would be able to introduce aids to encourage private storage of beef and veal. Also the variable premium system would become a permanent feature of beef market support arrangements when market prices are below 90 per cent of the guide price, to raise market returns to a level equal to 90 per cent of the guide price. The premium would be wholly financed by FEOGA. The final proposal, in the case of a very weak market, was the introduction of intervention buying by official EEC agencies. This would be as a last resort because buying does not stimulate demand, and the stored meat would lose quality.

The intervention price would therefore be set at levels below 90 per cent of the guide price.

Variable premiums were included in the 1978/79 price agreement. Other features of the proposals were not acted upon, and should now be considered to have been put aside, at least temporarily.

6. *Sheep meat*

There is no common EEC policy on sheep meat. The only regulations are with regard to trade with third countries, as agreed by the EEC within GATT. Individual nations are allowed to apply their own support measures. France, for example, restricts imports to support the domestic producer. In the UK there is a deficiency payment system when the market price falls below a fixed guaranteed level.

In April 1978 the EEC Commission put forward proposals for the common organization of the EEC sheep meat market. The Council of Ministers would agree annually a basic price for sheep meat with provision being made for seasonal adjustments to the basic price.   If the actual average market prices for sheep meat, as represented by a reference price, should fall below 90 per cent of the basic price, aid would be provided to encourage private storage of sheep meat. There would be no intervention purchases by official EEC agencies.

To control imports from non-EEC countries, a system of variable levies might be introduced for certain categories of sheep and sheep meat to replace the Common Customs Tariff. This would raise import prices to the basic price.

The Council of Ministers would have the power to grant a premium to sheep meat producers as and when it was thought to be required.

The proposals were rejected by France in June 1978 because it was thought that they would allow free access to the French market for New Zealand lamb. The United Kingdom attitude is that at least a 5 year transitional period is necessary to close the difference between the high level of market prices in France and the low level in the UK. So for the present at least there will continue to be no common organization of the market.

7. *Potatoes*

In March 1976 the Commission submitted proposals for a common market in potatoes. These were rejected by the Council of Ministers, which asked the Commission to reformulate and resubmit the proposals. At the time of writing this has not yet been done.

The 1976 proposal suggested the formation of a market similar to that operating for fruit and vegetables. Producer groups were to have been encouraged to apply common rules for the production and marketing of potatoes. Private storage aid was to be granted to recognized groups, if it was thought that supply was likely to considerably exceed demand.

Import controls suggested included using reference prices for new potatoes calculated on the basis of market prices realized in production areas in previous years, plus the costs of transportation from production areas to consumption areas, to represent the price at which new potatoes could be imported without being charged a levy. Entry prices would also be calculated for non-EEC member countries to bring import prices into line with reference prices.

The proposal was found to be unsatisfactory mainly because some EEC member states already operated market-control arrangements and the proposal was not considered to offer any improvement to these.

Monetary arrangements affecting farmers

Article 40 of the Treaty of Rome decrees that 'any common price policy shall be based on common criteria and uniform methods of calculation'. To this end prices specified within CAP have always been quoted in terms of the EEC's unit of account (UA) created in 1962. The unit of account is used in all the financial aspects of the EEC. It is, however, a notional currency, existing only on paper. When the UA was introduced it was not considered likely that the rates of exchange of individual Community currencies against the dollar and against each other would ever alter. This quickly proved to be an erroneous assumption.

Difficulties in the operation of common pricing, and hence the use of units of account, have occurred whenever a national currency has changed its parity against other currencies, or its rate of exchange has been allowed to float, because although Community budgets are calculated in terms of units of account, payments are made in the currencies of the member countries. Any possible solution to this situation will have unfortunate side effects.

The first disruption of the money market in EEC countries came in 1969 when the French franc was devalued and the German mark revalued upwards. As things stood France's domestic food prices would increase, and prices paid to German farmers would decrease, because the units of account were fixed in terms of US dollars. To avoid this the EEC allowed both countries to realign their currencies with UAs in steps, and until then temporary measures were adopted. For the devaluing countries imports were subsidized and exports taxed while for the revaluing countries imports were taxed and exports were subsidized. So in part of 1969/70 a green franc and a green mark were in existence whose values in terms of units of account did not equal the market rates of exchange but which were used to convert EEC farm prices in francs and marks. To prevent profits being made from trade between member countries, taxes or subsidies were applied to trade involving a state whose currency value had changed. These payments were termed monetary compensatory amounts (MCAs), and at first were fixed in nature, because the change in currency value was by a set amount, the French devaluation by 11.1 per cent and the German revaluation by 9.2 per cent.

The next monetary crisis came in 1971, when Germany, Belgium, and Luxemburg all floated their currencies while the US dollar's convertibility into gold was suspended. Because of this the MCAs adopted to bridge the gap between green rates and market rates of exchange were now variable in character, changing as the floating currencies changed. The 1971 crisis was resolved by the Smithsonian Agreement in which the US dollar was devalued, and other countries, including all EEC members agreed to limit the margins of fluctuation between their currencies to plus or minus 2.25 per cent. This was known as the tunnel.

Three months later the EEC restricted this even further, the maximum difference between the strongest and weakest EEC currency was restricted to 2¼ per cent, with the existing margins of plus or minus 2.25 per cent against the US dollar being maintained. These two constraints together were known as 'the snake in the tunnel'. This left two sets of exchange rates—green rates for CAP purposes, and real rates for normal international transactions. Variable MCAs were therefore still necessary. In 1973 the US dollar came under pressure again and was devalued from 0.921 SDRs to 0.829 SDRs. The Special Drawing Right (SDR) is an accounting device used internationally and administered by the International Monetary Fund (IMF). The EEC countries maintained the parity of the UA with the SDRs and, therefore, revalued against the dollar. They also pulled out of the tunnel agreement, and renamed the snake agreement as the joint float—the EEC currencies were free to float jointly against 11 third country currencies.

In mid 1973 the MCA system was revised and simplified. One UA was made equal to one SDR, which was in turn related to the currencies of the EEC countries by the agreement to limit currency fluctuations between EEC countries to a 2.25 per cent band. For each joint float country the central market rate and the green rate were fixed, therefore the MCA was fixed. The UK, Ireland, and Italy floated independently and retained variable MCAs. Currency valuation within the EEC has remained a major problem. The only way to prevent green rates from becoming wildly out of line with normal rates of exchange has been to devalue, from time to time, green rates which seriously diverge from real rates.

The value of green money is initially established by each national government at a level close to that of the value of its normal commercial currency. It is then maintained at a fixed parity and does not change with normal market fluctuations. If the value of the normal commercial currency begins to deviate from the green value, the national government is expected to adjust its fixed green rate. However, as any change is the responsibility of each government, it can be used for political purposes. In the UK, for example, the value of the green pound has been manipulated at times to hold down retail food prices.

When the UK joined the EEC in 1973 the green rate of exchange was fixed at £1 = 2.1644 UA, very close to the market exchange rate for the pound, £1 = 2.1598 UA. Since then the real value of the pound has fluctuated, mainly in a downward direction, and the reference rate of the green pound has been readjusted on a number of occasions.

Compensatory amounts are basically designed to take account of changes in relative values of member states' currencies which could, if uncorrected, lead to distortions in inter-state trading. Without any corrective measures it would be possible to export UK barley to Germany at a much lower price than that ruling on the German market, undercutting the German market and depressing prices, while at the same time forcing up UK prices because of a shortage created there.

MCAs are levies on exports from countries with lower valued currencies to those with higher valued currencies, and subsidies on imports for countries with weaker currencies. MCAs are paid to, or claimed from, the EEC farm fund. Because the pound has traditionally been a weak currency, relative to most EEC currencies, and the green pound reference rate remained unchanged for considerable periods of time, the UK has been able to claim heavy subsidies from the EEC farm fund.

Events in 1979 showed the effect on British agriculture of a vast reduction in MCAs. A stronger pound, coupled with devaluations of the green pound, brought the values of the pound and the green pound into approximate balance, and thus did away with the need for monetary compensatory amounts to create parity.

Accessionary compensatory amounts are sums of money designed to bridge the gap between high official EEC prices and the lower prices normally operating in the member countries at the time of their entry to the Community. A period of transition to full member status is agreed and ACAs are reduced each year in roughly equal steps as domestic prices increase and become in line with those of other member countries. Great Britain negotiated a 5-year period of transition, and ACAs operated until 1 January 1978 when official prices reached the same level as those in the rest of the EEC. In effect, ACAs act as border taxes between the new member and the other members to allow commodities to be traded competitively.

Effects of the operation of CAP on farmers

Having introduced the rudimentary concepts of Common Agricultural Policy, the remainder of this chapter will be devoted to considering the effects of the operation of the policy on farmers. Two major areas will be covered in turn, the mechanics of intervention buying, and implications for intra-community trade. To conclude the chapter a review will be made of the impact of the possible expansion of EEC membership and the various proposals for the reform of CAP which have been suggested from time to time.

1. *Intervention buying*

Intervention buying is an aspect of CAP which is of major interest to many farmers, because of its central importance to the marketing of their output. However, it is at the same time something which is very little understood, mainly because, to date, very little recourse has been made in the United Kingdom to intervention buying as a means of market support.

The mechanics of intervention buying as they operate in the cereals markets will be considered in depth, as an example of an operation which is reasonably common for all agricultural commodities. At any time the farmer can consider selling his grain into intervention as an alternative to selling through the normal channels. The standard intervention price is published, and selling into intervention obviously becomes an attractive proposition when market prices fall near to, or below, the standard intervention price.

Cereals intervention in the UK applies to breadmaking wheat, non-breadmaking wheat, and barley only. EEC regulations do not provide for intervention buying of oats and the UK trade in home-grown rye and maize is regarded as insufficient to warrant their inclusion in the scheme.

Offers of non-breadmaking wheat and barley can be made at any time and must be made in writing on the appropriate form and submitted to one of the Home Grown Cereals Authority's Regional Cereals Officers. There are 22 intervention centres in the UK and grain offered into intervention must be for delivery to a centre nominated by the seller from among the three nearest to the place where the grain is lying at the time of offer.

When a formal offer of a specific tonnage of feed wheat or barley is made, an acknowledgement will be sent to the farmer giving details of the intervention store to which the grain is to be delivered. In many cases the store will not be at the nominated intervention centre. If it is not, the price paid to the farmer will be the published intervention price adjusted on the basis of haulage costs (determined according to an official scale) to the point of actual delivery. The seller will also be given the starting and finishing dates of the period within which deliveries must be completed. The seller has two working days following the receipt of the acknowledgement of the offer in which to withdraw if he wishes; otherwise the offer becomes binding. The delivery period is at the option of the Intervention Board but will normally start during the month in which the grain is offered.

The farmer is responsible for arranging transport of his grain to the designated intervention store and for meeting the haulage costs. On delivery, each load will be sampled and tested to assess its quality characteristics. Although under certain circumstances limited tolerances are allowed, any individual load which is below the minimum quality permitted for intervention will be rejected. When the total quantity of grain has been delivered the final quality characteristics of the whole consignment will be calculated and a weighted average determined.

In their own interests, sellers into intervention should ensure that they meet, at least, the minimum quality standards, before offering to sell into intervention. Otherwise they may be involved in the expense of hauling grain to and from an intervention store without making a sale, in addition to paying the costs incurred at the store.

Once the grain has been accepted into intervention the exact price payable can be calculated. This depends on:

(i)   the date of the start of the delivery period;
(ii) the intervention centre nominated by the offerer;
(iii) the location of the intervention store stipulated by the Authority;
(iv) the location of the grain at the time of offer (where more than one parcel of grain is included in a single offer the location of the largest parcel is the relevant location);
(v)   the quality of the grain.

The basic price to be paid will be that in force during the month in which the delivery period fixed by the Authority started; it represents a delivered price at the nominated intervention centre. Where the delivery is required to a store which is *not* the nominated centre (or where grain is taken *in situ*), the price will be increased or reduced by reference to standard haulage cost scales to reflect any difference in haulage costs. Finally, the price will be adjusted to cover differences between the quality characteristics of the consignment, and the EEC Standard Quality. Premia are paid for grain of lower moisture content or higher specific weight and deductions are made for grain having a lower specific weight or a higher proportion of miscellaneous impurities or grain impurities within certain maxima.

Once the whole consignment has been received at the intervention store, full details of the exact quantity and quality of the grain taken over can be determined. The farmer will then be sent a form on which to claim for the quantity delivered. Payment will be made after this claim has been signed and returned to the Home-Grown Cereals Authority.

From this outline it can be seen that selling into intervention is one marketing option which is open to the farmer; however, it is an option which must be used with care. Delivering the grain can be very costly to the farmer if the grain fails to satisfy the minimum quality or quantity standards. It is also very likely that the net price which will be received by the farmer is not the same as the price announced for 'standard quality grain'.

EEC Regulations define 'standard qualities' for wheat, barley, and oilseed rape. Adjustments are made to intervention prices to reflect differences between the quality of the grain, as delivered into intervention, and the standard quality. 'Standard quality' should not be confused with 'minimum intervention quality'.

Standard quality grain is defined as being of sound and fair marketable quality, free from abnormal smell and live pests, of a colour proper to the grain and of a quality corresponding to the average quality of grain harvested under normal conditions in the EEC. It must meet requirements covering moisture content, specific weight, sprouted grains, grain impurities, miscellaneous impurities, broken grains, and oil content.

If the grain offered into intervention differs from the standard quality requirement then various premia and discounts will be applied to the intervention price. Bonuses always apply in respect of moisture content. The drier the grain, the greater will be the premium paid to the farmer. So far as specific weight is concerned either bonuses or discounts may apply, and for variations in impurities price adjustments are always either zero or negative. Both bonuses and discounts are calculated as percentages of the basic intervention price.

The largest possible bonus which can be obtained for exceptionally good grain of all types if 5.5 per cent, whilst the largest possible discount for grain which only just meets minimum intervention requirements is 6.25 per cent for feed wheat, 4.25 per cent for barley, and 5.0 per cent for breadmaking wheat. In addition to this the farmer must also include the cost of delivering the grain to the intervention centre. All in all the standard intervention price gives only a rough guide to the price likely to be received by the farmer, and selling to intervention is a marketing option which is likely to be most attractive to the farmer who is prepared to meet rigorous quality standards in the production of his arable crops, once again emphasizing the importance of considering marketing from the very beginning of production.

The net result is that in practice when market prices fall to intervention levels there is no rush by farmers to sell into intervention. Clearly the merits or otherwise of selling into intervention will vary enormously from individual to individual. The level below the intervention price to which the ex-farm price must fall before selling into intervention becomes viable will vary according to the seller's location and the grain quality. In exceptional circumstances this break-even ex-farm price could be almost as high as the intervention price itself for good quality grain located close to an intervention centre. On the other hand, for poor quality grain located a long distance from an intervention centre it could be as much as £8 or £10 below the intervention price.

To date there has been little experience in the UK on which to base conclusions as to the level to which the published average ex-farm price must fall before intervention selling takes place. In years when the EEC standard quality approximates to the average quality of grain sold, and if the discounts and bonuses for variations from this quality accurately reflect market differences, it would be reasonable to suppose that selling into intervention would be triggered when the market (ex-farm) price falls to the intervention price less average transport costs of between £2 and £3 per tonne. The more the ex-farm price falls below this level, the more intervention selling would take place, because for more people the intervention price would be above the break-even market price. Clearly in years when the average quality of grain is poor the trigger point would be correspondingly lower relative to the intervention price.

At present, the level to which market prices must fall before intervention selling takes place in the UK is also likely to be lower until farmers become more confident in the working of the system. Once this uncertainty is removed, the price trigger point is likely to increase nearer to the intervention price.

One final factor which is often of interest to the farmer is the cost of operating intervention support. The most recent information available for the UK refers to the 1978 calendar year. For that year total UK expenditure attributable to intervention activity was £49 million. In the cereals sectors, total expenditure by FEOGA was £58.3 million, practically all in the form of direct payments. Intervention costs were only £140 000, which was to be expected since little grain had been sold in this way because cereals prices had been generally buoyant throughout the year. The direct payments are mainly attributable to export refunds, reflecting the emphasis given to the disposal of surplus grain outside the Community during the year. The other major source of support was production subsidy payments for cereals used for manufacturing starch and in brewing, mainly for maize used in starch production.

2. *Implications for intra-community trade*

Since it is the basic principle of the market element of CAP that farm goods may move freely within the Community, it follows that, in principle, the scope for intra-community trade is unlimited for produce included in the provisions of the Treaty of Rome. This has important implications for the marketing of agricultural produce. Marketing-orientated farmers have a greatly expanded possible market for their output, although, in practice, the potential for trade depends to a great extent on geographical location and the relative strengths and weaknesses of the currencies of the member countries.

In the United Kingdom the major commodities affected by intra-community trade are fresh vegetables, milk products, potatoes, and livestock. Entry into the Community created a number of problems for UK horticultural producers. Full transition to membership means that domestic producers are vulnerable to competition from countries with lower costs of production. Between 1975 and 1977 imports, by volume, of fresh vegetables increased by 20 per cent. There has been a particular interest in the UK market from the Brittany area. Fresh vegetables brought across on the regular cross-channel ferries arrive in the UK in prime condition and are therefore in direct competition with home produce.

While this is unpopular with domestic producers it is entirely within the provisions of CAP, which is intended to encourage production in areas most suitable for particular commodities, and discourage production in less suitable areas.

A slightly different situation applies to trade in milk products. There is a basic difference in consumption patterns of milk throughout the Community. The UK alone consumes a significant proportion of its production as liquid milk, and has a doorstep delivery service which is unrivalled throughout the member countries. The whole distribution system is geared to large scale sales of bottled milk delivered by the milk roundsman. As a result the market is particularly vulnerable to imports of UHT milk from other member countries, designed to be sold through supermarkets at fiercely competitive prices.

At the present time imports of liquid milk are effectively curtailed by complex health and hygiene regulations. Already the regulations have been challenged by a French dairy co-operative in 1979, and the UK closed market was supported by the European Court of Justice. However, this support is only for a limited time to enable Community health and hygiene regulations to be harmonized. Should this market protection be removed then the future pattern of milk products marketing in the UK will be highly uncertain.

One market where import controls have been removed recently is that for potatoes. Prior to full membership, the UK banned all imports of main crop potatoes apart from in exceptional circumstances. This gave a floor to the market. However, the import ban was found to be in contravention of Community laws and was therefore removed in early 1979. As a result there is now a free market for potatoes.

The early indications are that this is unlikely to have a major effect on the returns enjoyed by potato producers. Potatoes do not travel well, and are a bulky crop and therefore expensive to transport. Limited tonnages have been imported, and the most serious competition to domestic production is likely to come from Holland, where there is a developed export trade for ware potatoes which can in some years exceed 1 million tonnes. One result of the open market is likely to be an increase in the importance of quality production. Sub-standard produce is unlikely to have a market since consumers and processors will undoubtedly prefer higher quality foreign imports.

There is also a limited export market for potatoes, particularly when prices are depressed in the UK. In the 1978-9 marketing year, about 30 000 tonnes of potatoes were exported to a number of countries, including the Middle East. Trade is therefore two way, although the balance will almost always favour imports.

Trade in livestock varies greatly, depending on the type of animal. At the present time, in the absence of an EEC sheep-meat policy, individual countries are allowed to operate their own market controls. UK producers have a particular interest in the French market since demand there is in excess of domestic supply. The French, however, for various reasons frequently close their sheep-meat market and have an exclusive trading treaty with the Republic of Ireland. This would appear to be in contravention to the Community spirit and has been challenged by the UK government. Should a common market be introduced for sheep-meat then the intra-community trade prospects should be reasonably favourable to British producers.

There is already a substantial trade in live cattle within the Community. There has been a strong French demand for British-bred dairy cattle, which has resulted in large scale exports over the past few years. Many of the export cattle have been used to restock farms which have suffered brucellosis breakdowns, and other buyers have opted for British dairy breeds to replace established Normande herds. There seems to be little reason why this trade should not continue in the future.

Reform of the Common Agricultural Policy

There have been, over time, proposals from many quarters, suggesting various changes to CAP. All have the common base of attempting to improve the efficiency of the common market for farm produce, and some of the more recent are reviewed now.

In 1973 the Wageningen Memorandum considered the problem of relative prices. This suggestion followed economic principles in as much as products in short supply should receive price increases whilst those in surplus should either have prices cut, or be held stable as general inflation proceeds. It was proposed that the price of grains should be stabilized and this should be coupled with policy measures designed to stimulate beef production. In 1979 a similar policy was introduced with dairy product prices being frozen in an endeavour to reduce surplus production.

An alternative proposal put forward by Josling (1973) involved reductions in the prices of grains and possibly dairy products, accompanied by indirect supplementation. This was, in effect, a return to the UK system of deficiency payments. One advantage of this system was that the cost of food would be reduced either directly or indirectly.

In 1977 Marsh (1977*a, b*) put forward two alternative proposals for reform of Common Agricultural Policy. Two long-term policy alternatives are suggested to overcome the Community's problem of long-term structural surpluses.

The first proposal suggests that the Community should agree annually the maximum amount of money it is prepared to spend to finance intervention purchases and export refunds. The advantages of this are seen to be:

(i)   a ceiling would be placed on the budgetary liability of the Community;
(ii) a real deterrent would be introduced against surplus production, without exposing farmers to the dangers of excessive price movements in an uncontrolled market;
(iii) a return to placing increased importance on demand and supply factors in balancing the market.

The second plan provides for an annual agreement by the Council of Ministers of common community trading prices at which agricultural products would be traded within the boundaries of the Community. Member countries would then be free to manage, or fix, their own internal prices as they wished. Each country would be responsible for taxing or subsidizing the commodities traded, to make up the difference between its own natural price levels and the Community trading prices.

To avoid chronic overproduction a quota system might be used. Alternatively, the Council of Ministers could agree to lower the relevant Community trading price, increasing the cost to Member States with producer prices above the Trading Price, of supporting through subsidies the production and sale of excess supplies.

The major benefit claimed for this proposal is a saving in costs, because the system of representative rates of exchange and monetary compensatory amounts would be unnecessary. At the same time it is possible that effective steps to limit surpluses might also be taken.

All of these proposals stem from a desire to improve the manageability of CAP. It is possible, however, that future changes in the composition of the membership of the Community will necessitate reform of agricultural policy. At present, further enlargement of the European Community is in prospect, this time from nine to twelve members, as a result of applications from Greece, Spain, and Portugal.

In principle, the Community has responded favourably to their membership applications. It is likely, however, that there will be considerable problems to be overcome, if the size of the Community does increase. The major area of difficulty will almost certainly be agriculture, since this industry has a far more important role in the countries applying than in the existing member countries. In basic terms the accession of Spain, Portugal, and Greece would mean that the number of people working in agriculture would go up by 55 per cent, the number of farm holdings would increase by 57 per cent, and the agricultural area by 49 per cent. However, because agricultural productivity is backward in all three countries, production would only increase by 25 per cent.

The applicant countries all expect considerable economic gains from CAP. On the budgetary level, the finance of agricultural policy becomes a Community responsibility, and market price support measures would be entirely financed by FEOGA. Commodities likely to be most seriously affected by the increased production levels are wine, olive oil, and certain horticultural products, particularly tomatoes, grapes, apples, pears, peaches, and apricots. Should the enlarged Community become a reality some reform of agricultural policy will be inevitable to produce solutions to problems which are, above all, social, regional, and structural.

Part III. Marketing channels used by farmers

6. Channels used by farmers marketing individually

Introduction

In the first part of this book a review has been undertaken of the relevance of marketing in the particular environment of agricultural businesses. The overall conclusion of this review was that, although marketing is carried out in agriculture, not all of the participants in the markets, namely farmers, are personally involved in the marketing of their output. In the second part relevant legislation affecting agricultural marketing was discussed. The aim of this third part of the book is to investigate, in detail, the various methods by which farmers dispose of their produce. Various well tried and tested channels have been used throughout generations by farmers, and the most important of these will be considered from the point of view of their use for particular commodities, and their individual advantages and disadvantages.

Such a consideration is relevant, because all farmers must utilize marketing channels, regardless of whether they are production orientated or marketing orientated, so long as they produce goods which are in excess of their domestic consumption. So any farmer at above subsistence level will be required to choose between various marketing channels in order to dispose of his produce. For some this is simply a matter of routine, selling through the same outlets year in and year out; however, for others the choice of marketing channel is a very important decision. Certainly there exist possibilities for the marketing-orientated farmer to improve his profit potential, if he is prepared to spend time deliberating over which marketing channel to use, and then makes his decision on the basis of sound economic motives.

Specific product trends

It is claimed, for example, that there are certain well-defined product trends which can be examined by the marketing-orientated farmer, regardless of his choice of marketing channel, to see whether he can make an increased profit from a knowledgeable utilization of such patterns. In order to illustrate this situation, four commodities: milk, livestock, potatoes, and cereals will be considered briefly in relation to the conditions facing British farmers.

1. *Milk*

There is a long-established situation of a lower supply of milk in winter than in summer, chiefly because of the greater costs involved in winter milk production. In order to balance the supply of milk throughout the year, the bodies co-ordinating milk distribution in the UK, the Milk Marketing Boards, offer prices for milk which are higher in winter than in summer. This is shown in Table 6.1

Table 6.1. Average prices paid to United Kingdom milk producers in pence per litre from 1977 to 1979

	1977	1978	1979	1977-9 Index
Apr.-Sept.	8.653	9.351	9.797	9.267
Oct.-Mar.	9.935	10.341	11.117	10.464

Source: MMB (1979).

The marketing-orientated farmer can compare the relative costs and benefits of summer and winter milk production and decide which is the most profitable system for him to undertake. Having arrived at this decision he can gear his production to match the profit-making opportunities.

2. *Livestock*

For livestock, there are certain traditional summer-winter relationships which are given a lot of publicity. For example, in beef production it is maintained that beef prices are lower in summer than in winter, because of the lower production in winter. However, analysis of the levels of production and prices month by month over a period of time for beef does not show this relationship so clearly. There is a distinct production pattern with low levels of supply from March to mid-July, and then high levels of supply from August to December. Prices show very little synchronization from year to year, although there is a general trend of high prices from March to May, along with a Christmas peak in December. In view of this uncertainty it is probably most important for the marketing-orientated farmer to know the price trends for his local auction market and match his production to meet higher prices. With a 2-3 year production cycle for beef, though, it is very hard to apply marketing considerations when the long-term price forecasts are so notoriously unreliable. So the beef producer can do very little long-term marketing unless he is prepared to enter into contract production and agree a price which will be held to regardless of market prices.

In pig production it is maintained that prices are lower in the summer for pork because there is less demand for the product, stemming from the old tradition of 'only eat pork when there is an 'R' in the month'. In this case analysis of the levels of production and prices month by month over time does show this relationship quite clearly. In summer demand is low, and prices are low. In winter demand is greater and prices are usually higher. The application of marketing orientation to pig production is, however, hampered by the unstable nature of the supply of pigs by the UK farmer. In general the UK pig producer is a price chaser, increasing his breeding herd as prices of pig meat go up, and running down the herd only when oversupply has forced prices right down. The result is the notorious pig cycle which makes any elaborate marketing analysis imprecise. The most profitable pig producer will be the efficient producer who can read the market signals correctly, stocking up just as prices and production reach their peak. This is known as producing against the cycle and requires a deal of expertise as well as a lot of luck. This is not helped by the manipulation of agricultural policy to favour consumers and, indirectly, importers of pig meat. There is also the related problem that if too many farmers read the market signals correctly and react as suggested, then the result could be a continuation of the spiral.

3. *Potatoes*

In potato production there is a general trend that prices rise towards the end of the year. There are also premia available for early production and for quality seed production. The marketing-orientated farmer is, therefore, faced with a variety of choices of production.

He can aim for an early lifting crop in the hope of catching high prices. The danger here, of course, is that the crop may not be fully matured, and so yields are likely to be lower than later lifted fields. Alternatively the farmer could aim for quality seed production. There is a difficulty here in that there are geographical limitations to possible seed growing areas. The third alternative is for the farmer to grow main crop potatoes and then store them over the winter in order to obtain higher prices in late spring of the next year. The danger with this system is that in some years the extra returns will not cover the increased costs of storage. So once again the individual farmer must make his decision on the grounds of his personal preferences and his local knowledge. This is a haphazard way of decision making and there is a real need for improved market intelligence, particularly accurate price forecasts over the year.

4. *Cereals*

In cereals production, prices vary over the year, with the UK domestic price being to a large extent affected by the size of the USA and the Russian grain harvests. Most farmers store their grain after harvest and then sell over the winter months, either as tradition dictates or when marketing considerations indicate that a sale should be made. Cereal marketing is perhaps the most developed branch of agriculture and there is real potential for the marketing-orientated farmer to organize his marketing throughout the year.

One possibility is for the farmer to engage in a contract for quality seed production. Here a definite premium will be available so long as rigorous quality regulations are maintained. Alternatively, the farmer can aim for the milling-wheat market, or the malting-barley market, the 'quality end' of the market, although caution must be exercised. Millers and the maltsters appear to have remarkably flexible definitions of milling and malting quality, depending on whether there is a glut or a shortage of potential supplies. Production specifically for this end of the market should only be undertaken if the farmer has a reliable contract signed, and has a good working relationship established with his merchant.

Reference to these four commodities shows the potential for farmers to consider particular facets of agricultural markets. The next step is to look in more detail at the particular marketing channels through which farmers dispose of their output. The nature of the outlets used varies according to the commodity being produced. In this chapter reference will be made to marketing channels which are used by farmers acting individually and the following two chapters will consider the channels which are available to farmers when they dispose of their produce in unison. Finally consideration will be given to possibilities for the farmer to bypass the normal marketing channels and market his produce directly to the consumer.

Channels used by farmers acting individually

By and large, when the farmer operates as an individual in the market, his ability to influence that market is negligible. Despite this disadvantage, the bulk of agricultural produce is marketed by farmers acting independently, through various outlets. Some of the most important of these are live auctions, private deadweight selling, and the use of agents, dealers, and wholesalers. These will, therefore, be considered in greater detail now.

1. *Auctions*

Auctions comprise an institution which has become deeply enmeshed in the tradition and history of British agriculture and it is thus a method of marketing which is of great significance. Auction selling originates from the traditional weekly market days or fairs held in towns and villages around the country and it has been formalized, under the direction of an accredited auctioneer who controls the sales of the commodity which is changing hands. The auction is, therefore, an organized method by which the ownership of some goods is transferred.

There are two major systems of auction which can be used. The traditional method used in the UK is one of upward bidding, where individuals offer bids of increasing value and the person who offers the final, and therefore highest, bid is the purchaser. Bidding in this style of auction is often very indistinct, perhaps a flicker of an eyelid, or a scratch of the nose, or a nod of a head. There is some psychology, or 'kidology', involved in bidding which can influence the final price which is realized.

The other major system of auction is known as the Dutch method which, although it is widely used on the Continent, has found little application in the UK. In a Dutch auction the auctioneer offers prices in a downward trend and the first person to bid makes the purchase. The system is occasionally referred to as a clock auction because the usual method of displaying the price suggested by the auctioneer is by the sweep hand of a clock located beside the auctioneer and controlled by him. Potential buyers are equipped with hand sets which enable them to stop the clock and thus make the purchase, simply by pressing a button. It is, therefore, a method of selling which lends itself to automation and it has been applied, on a state-wide basis, in the USA.

An experiment in the use of Dutch-auction techniques was undertaken by a farmer's co-operative in Gloucestershire in 1964. The move was part of the development of a new market complex and attracted Government grant aid. It utilized the mechanical clock system. However, it had to be withdrawn after only 9 months because of resistance from buyers and sellers. Buyers claimed that they could not see the produce at the time of sale and also that they found it difficult to adjust to falling prices. Sellers complained that they were not receiving competitive prices for their produce under the different auction system.

Auctions can be utilized for disposing of virtually any agricultural commodity, anything for which it is possible to find a bidder. In practice the major commodities to be offered for sale at auction markets are livestock. Farm sales also often utilize auction methods when the ownership of agricultural holdings is being transferred. This comprises both the holding itself and the live- and dead-stock of the farm in certain cases.

At an auction market each category of livestock is usually sold separately. Generally fat stock is sold on a value per weight basis. Store animals, that is animals sold before they are ready for slaughter, are normally sold on a value per head basis, although buyers may be given some indication of the weight of the animals. Animals may be sold singly, or in groups, depending on their nature, the wishes of the seller, and the custom of the market.

The transfer of ownership is controlled by an auctioneer who makes a valuation of the animal, accepts bids, and makes the final sale. He is the employee of the auction market and the final arbitrator in any dispute. To finance the running of the market a commission is charged to the seller of any animal passing through the market. The general tradition is for commission to be charged to the seller and not to the buyer. In addition value added tax is charged on the commission, but not on the sale itself.

There are various advantages and disadvantages associated with selling animals by auction. The major disadvantages are as follows:

1. It is difficult to make an accurate and consistent valuation of the current trade for a particular agricultural commodity. Trade may fluctuate throughout the day, and there is no guarantee that prices at different auction centres on the same day will equate.
2. There is a danger of buying 'a pig in a poke'. There is little opportunity of inspecting animals individually before purchase, and at times, if animals are sold in a group, there will be one concealed among them which is not of the same quality as the others.
3. There is a danger of buying rings being instituted. This occurs when buyers get together with the intention of sharing out purchases, thus reducing the intensity of competition. There is a greater danger of this occurring in small auction centres than in large markets where there are likely to be a greater number of buyers.

Conversely the advantages of auction selling are:

1. All buyers can see what is being sold, make their valuation of it, and it is known immediately how much the animal has made and who has bought it. It is a rapid and efficient method of transferring the ownership of large numbers of animals between willing buyers and sellers.
2. The average farmer takes great pride and satisfaction from selling animals at an auction market. The value of this can never be calculated quantitatively, however, it is of real value none the less.
3. On the whole, the auction system provides a fair system of valuation of produce handled through it, and operates in an efficient manner.

The major criticism levelled against the auction market is that it is an unnecessary link in the chain between the producer and the slaughterhouse. Many auction markets, however, provide a useful function as assembly and sorting points, leading to economies in transport costs by increasing the size of subsequent long-distance loads.

The number of auction markets operating in Great Britain has declined consistently over the last 10 years, as illustrated in Table 6.2

Table 6.2. Number of auction markets in Great Britain from 1968 to 1978

	1968	1974	1976	1978
England and Wales	453	369	354	332
Scotland	74	65	65	65

Source: Meat and Livestock Commission, Unpublished statistics[†].

This has quite considerable implications for the livestock industry, with the trend being more pronounced in certain parts of Britain than in others. The markets which have closed tend to have been the small-scale centres situated in areas of high population density. The proximity of population centres reduces the collection function of the auction market. Also markets were traditionally situated in the centre of towns, and therefore occupied prime sites with high development value. This coupled with difficulties of access for large transport units has resulted in an increase in the importance of large, purpose-built auction centres, well situated in terms of infrastructure requirements and providing a large range of facilities. Markets such as those at Shrewsbury, Oswestry, and Banbury in Great Britain are good examples.

This is confirmed by the work of Thomas and Bateman (1973) who suggest that trends in England and Wales indicate a prosperous long-term future for markets with a throughput of more than 20 000 cattle units per annum. Conversely, the number of markets with a throughput of less than 10 000 cattle units per annum is expected to diminish.

The markets of the future are envisaged as large scale, well-equipped regional centres, serving larger areas than those they will supercede. It is interesting to note, however, that Inman[‡] in a study of prices at two auction centres, one large scale and one small scale,

[†]The author is extremely grateful to Archie Sains, of the Meat and Livestock Commission, for the compilation of data used in tables throughout this chapter.
[‡]Inman, D. (1976). The role and efficiency of the livestock auction in the marketing of fatstock. Unpublished B.Sc. Dissertation, University of Nottingham.

found no consistent price advantage to encourage sales through the large scale centre, with each market attracting different types of buyer.

2. *Deadweight selling*

The major alternative method available in Great Britain for transferring the ownership of animals is deadweight selling. This involves an evaluation of the worth of an animal on a deadweight, rather than a liveweight basis. It is a method of marketing which is usually incorporated with some form of contract production, considered in greater depth in Chapter 9. It is claimed that deadweight selling gives a surer market than the live auction, with fewer fluctuations in trade; it certainly provides a viable alternative. The problem always exists, however, similar to that at the live auction, of how the trade should be set, that is, who decides how much should be paid per kilogram. Often prices are related to the current liveweight trade, creating a definite link between the two methods of marketing.

The proportions of animals which are sold by liveweight and deadweight vary according to the type of animal. Information is available only for certified fatstock passing through marketing channels and Table 6.3 shows the changes which have occurred over the last 20 years.

The data in Table 6.3 shows that the auction system has more than held its own in the number of fat cattle and sheep sold. However, any conclusions must be treated with caution as they refer only to certified animals, and comparisons with previous years for the sale of pigs are meaningless because of the severe SVD restrictions imposed on the industry in the mid-1970s.

Over the past 15-20 years there has been a definite trend towards an increase in the proportion of fat cattle sold deadweight, however, progress has been slow and since the mid-1970s the percentage of certified cattle passing through liveweight auctions has ceased to decline, stabilising at around 51-52 per cent. The reasons for this situation are many and complex. The main advantage of the deadweight system is that farmers are paid for the carcass they produce, rather than on the liveweight buyer's assessment of how well the animal will kill out. This advantage, however, is not always sufficient to encourage producers to change from their traditional method of marketing, or to forego the option to withdraw their stock if the price is not right.

Table 6.3. Certification of fatstock by various marketing methods in England and Wales from 1954 to 1976

	Auction (%)	Private liveweight (%)	Ordinary deadweight (%)	Bacon factories (%)
1954-55				
Cattle	73.0	5.0	22.0	—
Sheep	65.5	5.2	29.3	—
Pigs	26.5	0.5	24.0	49.0
1964-65				
Cattle	69.0	3.4	27.6	—
Sheep	61.4	4.6	34.0	—
Pigs	18.0	0.5	30.5	51.0
1972-73				
Cattle	51.0	0.9	48.1	—
Sheep	60.7	2.2	37.1	—
Pigs	12.8	0.2	41.6	45.5
1975-6				
Cattle	51.1	0.7	48.2	—
Sheep	64.9	1.6	33.5	—
Pigs	10.4	0.1	48.0	41.5

Source: Meat and Livestock Commission, Unpublished statistics.

Another factor is the speed of payment. Producers are paid immediately by the auction market, whereas it may take 1-2 weeks if the animals are sold by deadweight. The existence of national, and independent, carcass classification schemes, which could possibly be adopted as the basis of deadweight pricing, was expected to increase the interest of buyers in deadweight transactions. It was also aimed to facilitate trading in carcass meat with retailers and other meat buyers, as meat could be ordered, in classification terms, by telephone, in the certainty that meat of the precise description would be delivered. Classification has, in fact, encountered considerable opposition, some wholesalers believing that they would receive a glut of orders for one particular type of carcass and would be unable to dispose of carcasses of less desirable classification. An advantage of the liveweight auction is that it can dispose of all kinds of qualities of animals and in fulfilling this role cannot refuse to accept animals which do not conform to quality specifications, this, of course, being to the producer's advantage.

The last 10 years have seen a decline, not only in the number of livestock auction markets, but also in the number of deadweight killing centres. In 1968 there were 2300 slaughterhouses in the UK, by 1976 the number had declined to 1500, of which the largest 90 were responsible for 60 per cent of the total killings, with the smallest 900 slaughtering only 2 per cent of the total kill. It is these slaughterhouses which are disappearing at the fastest rate. The two major types of slaughterhouse to disappear are those operated privately by individual butchers, and those provided by local authorities. Increased health restrictions as a result of EEC membership have resulted in their non-viability as profit making units, and they are tending to be replaced by modern, large scale centres, operated by four major types of organization:

(i)   units operated by meat retailing firms such as Dewhursts, Baxters, and Matthews;

(ii)   units operated by meat importers, as a result of the swing towards a greater reliance on home-produced food. Importers are mainly buying up existing centres rather than building new ones;

(iii) units run by pseudo-farmers' groups such as Farmark. The majority of cases have shown that there is very little profit to be gained from meat wholesaling;

(iv)   some units have been taken over by farmers' groups and co-operatives such as Buchan Beef, North Devon Meat, and Welsh Quality Lamb.

Historically, central meat markets played a very important role in the distribution and marketing of carcass meats, providing a centre where meat could go after it left the slaughterhouse. Now, as a result of the developments previously outlined, they are tending to become clearing houses for lower quality produce, which otherwise would not find a ready market. The central markets were traditionally a very accurate indicator of market trends and wholesale prices, but this has ceased to be the case.

There are various arguments raised concerning the relative merits of liveweight and deadweight marketing of farm animals. In favour of liveweight assessment it is said that the buyer in this situation can assess the *eatability* of the meat more accurately than the buyer who sees only the carcass. It is suggested that the buyer cannot only see the breed and age of the animal, but can in addition see how and where it has been fed. On the other hand, when considering *cutability*, it is claimed that the liveweight buyer has to estimate the killing out percentage, which can vary greatly between apparently similar animals. The deadweight buyer, however, can judge the actual weight of the carcass, and will know more accurately the proportions of bones, fat and more, or less, desirable cuts in the carcass.

It is generally accepted that the *eatability* and *cutability* characteristics of meat can be judged more satisfactorily from the carcass than from the live animal. If the assessments made at the auction are less precise than those made on a deadweight basis, it follows that the auction is likely to be a less precise indicator of trade preferences to the producer. The auction relies entirely on the price mechanism to transmit the preferences of the consumer and the trade to the producer. It is difficult, however, for the producer to separate the degree to which the price he receives is affected by the quality of the animal, and the degree of influence of general price levels.

Auctions are said to provide the marketing system with a great deal more flexibility in dealing with fluctuations in supply than does deadweight selling, where, once the animal is dead it becomes a perishable commodity. It has been suggested, by the Joint English and Scottish Livestock Auctioneers Committee in 1962 (Verdon Smith 1964) that the right to withdraw an animal from the auction ring is exercised to an extent which is sufficient to have an effect on prices, contributing to stability by putting a bottom on the market. The deadweight system is less flexible, although deadweight buyers can phase their offtake from farms in order to even out supplies, or store the meat in times of glut.

Price determination is possibly the most crucial aspect of livestock marketing. The main mechanism for determining prices at a first hand level is the fatstock auction market. Even buyers purchasing on a deadweight basis state that they use auction prices as an indicator, generally the principal indicator for their price schedules. Verdon Smith reported that the Ministry of Agriculture, Fisheries, and Food found that, as far as the UK market was concerned, a comparison of movements in the average national weekly market prices and the national supply of certified stock suggested that, in broad terms, market prices reflect long-term variations in supply and not usually short-term fluctuations. This comparison of week-to-week changes supports the view that the auction system has absorbed and dampened down many of the very pronounced short-term fluctuations in supplies (which for cattle can be as high as 20-30 per cent from week to week). These supply fluctuations have not been reflected in price changes of similar proportions. Differences in price occur from market to market, these variations being due to local supply and demand situations, quality differences, local preferences, and remoteness of the area served. In 1962-3 the Ministry of Agriculture, Fisheries, and Food extracted supply and price data over a period for a number of markets. Substantial fluctuations in supply occurred from week to week with short-term movements away from the national trend, although prices remained relatively more stable than supply, broadly reflecting national trends. Thus prices remain more stable than supply, shielding the producer from short term or local market fluctuations and providing a considerable degree of stability in the price of a product which fluctuates in supply and is perishable. In the long run, prices have reflected supplies nationally. The general conclusion on pricing at the fatstock auction is that the auction provides, within the limits of its ability to distinguish quality, a reasonably satisfactory pricing mechanism.

More recently Bateman, Kerr, Owen, and Thomas (1971) in a study of the structure of livestock marketing in Wales, examined the level of concentration of purchasing amongst major buyers in the auction. The measure of concentration used was the five firm concentration ratio, i.e. the proportion of purchases accounted for by the five largest buyers. As can be seen in Table 6.4 a strong inverse relationship was found between buyer concentration and market size.

Almost two-thirds of markets in size group 1, which sold fat cattle, had a buyer concentration of 100 per cent for fat cattle. In size group 4 buyer concentration drops significantly for fatstock, probably due to the importance of single and mutliple shop butchers as buyers in this size of auction. By contrast markets in groups greater than 4 have higher concentration levels, tending to be dominated by wholesalers.

Price differences were examined by Thomas and Bateman (1973). Fat cattle prices in Wales were found to be lower than prices in England. Analysis showed that distance from consuming centre

Table 6.4. Buyer concentration and auction market size
in Wales in 1969

Market size group	Market throughput in cattle units	Percentage bought by five largest buyers		
		Fat cattle	Fat sheep	Fat pigs
1	0-2499	100	100	95
2	2500-4999	80	75	85
3	5000-9999	90	80	84
4	10 000-19 999	50	55	55
5	20 000-39 999	55	65	65
7	80 000 and over	62	50	50

Source: Bateman *et al.* (1971).

is an important part of the explanation. In the annual marketing trough the price differentials were lower, and could be accounted for in this way, but in the peak marketing period Welsh prices were below expected levels after adjusting for transport costs. The remaining difference was thought to be explained in terms of the structure of the auction market, i.e. size and degree of buyer concentration. If was found that for several types of stock and in certain quarters of the year, there was a tendency for prices to be lower in small markets and in the ones of high buyer concentration. This relationship was found most frequently for the heavier (specialized demand) stock and in the less important marketing periods. For lighter stock in the peak marketing period, however, size of market and degree of buyer concentration did not explain the price differences which were in excess of transport costs; that is there was no evidence that the structure of the markets was the cause and it was probably that during the peak period the supply of stock was too great, relative to demand.

3. *Agents, dealers, and wholesalers*

Compared to auctions, the role of the agent is much less extensive in agriculture. Agents are rather more widely used in marketing to the farmer, as opposed to by the farmer, however they do have a place in certain specific circumstances. Basically the agent acts, as the name suggests, as a handler of agricultural produce, purchasing the produce from the farmer on behalf of some further link in the marketing chain, either on commission, or for a fee.

The major area in which agents operate in agricultural marketing is with regard to horticultural produce, handling the produce on behalf of producers for a commission. In this way farmers send their output to the agent at the fruit and vegetable market, who will find the best possible market for the produce in return for his commission. The farmer may set a reserve on his produce, and in the event of it remaining unsold the produce must be returned—at the farmer's expense—since the agent is only handling the produce, and does not actually own it.

Dealers differ from agents in that they actually take financial possession of the agricultural commodity in question before disposing of it. Dealers operate in various ways and tend to specialize in particular agricultural commodities. The livestock dealer, for example, may purchase his requirements from an auction market, or markets, or he may deal directly with his farmer customers. He will not purchase for his own consumption but will find a market, most importantly farmers who prefer to let a professional buy for them, trusting his judgement.

Dealers tend to be more numerous for non-livestock commodities. There are a large number of hay and straw merchants, for example, who buy from farmers and sell to farmers, providing a transport and delivery function in return for the difference between the buying and selling price. Similarly, for arable crops, there are a large number of dealers who purchase cereals from farmers and then sell them on to large manufacturers, or to other farmers who have a grain deficit.

Fruit and vegetable merchants also operate as dealers, as well as agents. This is the other major method of handling horticultural produce, with in this case the merchant actually purchasing the produce from the farmer and then selling it on to the greengrocer, supermarket, or whatever. This time if any produce remains unsold the responsibility does not lie with the farmer. In general, the more perishable commodities tend to be handled on an agency basis, and the less perishable commodities on a dealership basis. As a result of this, the producer carries the most extreme risks of trading, not the merchant.

Alexander (1960) has defined a wholesaler as follows, 'a business unit which buys and resells merchandise to retailers and other merchants and/or industrial, institutional and commercial users, but which does not sell in significant amounts to ultimate consumers.'

The chief function of the wholesaler is to assemble the output of many producers into an assortment which is of potential interest to buyers, and break their bulk so as to meet the scale of the need of the customer.

In agriculture the wholesaler plays an important part in the marketing of produce, usually existing as the next link in the chain after the auction market, dealer or whatever. In certain cases, however, the wholesaler acts as dealer or agent and so comes into direct contact with the farmer. This is the case, by and large, in fruit and vegetable production, with wholesalers acting as agents or dealers in their relationships with producers.

In livestock production the dealer may act as a small scale wholesaler, for example purchasing caste or geld cows to fulfil a contract with a local authority for meat for hospitals, schools, university halls of residence and so on. In other cases the farmer may deal directly with the wholesaler. A good example in the UK is the Fatstock Marketing Corporation (FMC) which purchases directly from the farmer and then fulfils a wholesaling function. Similarly a significant proportion of pork pigs in this country are sold on contract to a commercial firm which operates as a wholesaler, and also to a certain extent as a retailer as well.

7. Channels used by farmers acting in unison: statutory marketing organizations

Introduction

The obvious available alternative to marketing his produce as an individual, is for the farmer to join together with one or more other producers and for them to market their output collectively. There are two major ways in which this can take place. Either the Government can coerce the individual producer, or else individuals can co-operate voluntarily. Both situations have applied, and do apply in the agricultures of the majority of countries in the world.

One of the main aims of co-operation, both voluntary and compulsory, is to reduce the inherent weakness of the farmer who operates as an individual in the market, since the influence of the individual on the market is severely limited by the relative smallness of his scale of operations compared to the people with whom he is trading. It has long been held that if farmers act in the market, not as individuals, but co-operate in some way and market their produce in unison, then there will be synergistic returns available to such co-operation, because of the increased scale of operation.

Synergy is sometimes known as the '2 + 2 = 5 effect', and is said to have taken place when the combined returns on the firm's resources is greater than the sum of its parts. When farmers co-operate there is a pooling of a variety of resources, including management and marketing competence and know how. It is held that this pooling will result in an increase in the returns enjoyed by farmers for their output, although the actual extent of the increase is difficult to quantify.

Agricultural Marketing Boards

The Agricultural Marketing Acts of 1931 and 1933 provided for the preparation of statutory marketing schemes, which would become law if they were approved by Parliament, and by a sufficient majority of affected producers. The first Boards formed covered hops, potatoes, pigs, and milk, and since the end of the Second World War a number of Boards have been set up, some succeeding, and some enjoying less success.

Within this chapter consideration will be given, firstly to the establishment of Boards, secondly to the ways in which they work, and thirdly to the commodities for which Boards operate in the United Kingdom. Three commodities, milk, potatoes, and eggs will be considered in particular detail to show the varying degrees of success or failure of different types of Board. Finally the likely future role of Boards within the framework of Britain's membership of the European Economic Community will be analysed.

A Marketing Board can be defined (Metcalf 1969) as 'a producer controlled, compulsory, horizontal organisation, sanctioned by Governmental authority to perform specific marketing operations in the interests of the producers of the commodity concerned'. Control, therefore, lies with the producer, and once formed, the Marketing Board covers all producers of the commodity regardless of whether they voted in favour of its inception. The Board must be an amalgamation of farmers only, and should not include any other stages of the marketing chain. It cannot be formed without Parliamentary authority, and the operation of the Board must be laid down at the outset, only powers granted at this time can be used by the Board.

1. *Establishment of a Marketing Board*

In considering the formation of Marketing Boards for agricultural commodities in Great Britain one point must be stressed immediately. As a result of EEC Membership, it is relatively unlikely that any new Boards will be instituted unless there is a considerable change in the structure of Common Agricultural Policy. Having said that, the legislative machinery still exists to enable the creation of Boards and in 1979 considerable attention was given to the possibility of setting up a Board responsible for the marketing of Scottish seed potatoes.

The initial impetus for the creation of a Board must always come from producers of a commodity. In practice, the National Farmers Union has always been actively involved in the preparation of submissions to the Minister of Agriculture regarding the establishment of Boards. So long as the Minister is satisfied that the producers are representative of the industry, he publicizes the intentions of the proposed Board so that objections and comments regarding the scheme can be raised. In the light of any reactions, the Minister then consults the proposers of the scheme, taking account of any objections raised. If agreement is reached then a Marketing Board can be set up, otherwise a committee of enquiry is set up and the findings eventually submitted to Parliament. All these stages are designed to ensure that no Board can be put forward to which there are serious objections.

If a Board is set up, its first function is to compile a register of all producers of the commodity in question. A vote of registered producers is held, so that they can indicate their support or disapproval of the scheme. Under pre-EEC legislation, as long as 50 per cent of producers voted, and of those at least two thirds were in favour of the scheme, then the Board could be set up. As a result of EEC membership the conditions have been modified. For a Marketing Board for milk, for example, to be established, at least 80 per cent of producers who vote in a ballot must be in favour of the scheme, and those producers in favour must represent at least 50 per cent of milk production in the area to be covered by the Board.

Immediately after a Board has been set up it is reviewed by the Minister of Agriculture to determine whether the scheme will result in an overall improvement in the efficiency of both the production and marketing of the commodity concerned. Once a Board has been established then its compulsory powers apply to all producers, including those who did not vote in its favour. Producers must, therefore, comply with the regulations, or else cease production.

2. *Operation of Marketing Boards*

Marketing Board schemes contain powers to regulate the supply of a commodity and/or powers to trade in a commodity, depending on its type. Each agricultural commodity differs in terms of conditions of supply and demand, and marketing conditions vary considerably. Marketing Boards can have very wide ranging powers. They can, for example, lay down very strict conditions regarding the quality of production, they can also determine the price of the commodity, and control the channels of distribution.

When a Marketing Board is established it must set out in its submission the controls which it intends to utilize. Those powers alone can be used in the operation of the Board. If a Board wishes to extend or change its powers then a new submission must be made to the Minister of Agriculture, which must undergo the same procedure as the original applications.

Because the potential powers of a Marketing Board are so extensive various regulative committees are set up as safeguards to control their operation. A consumer committee is built into any agricultural marketing scheme. Consumers can object to any undesirable effect of a Board once it is in operation. In addition an *ad hoc* committee of investigation is established, which can examine the affairs of the Marketing Board. This is designed to reveal any inefficiencies or malpractices.

The major objective of a Marketing Board can be described as to improve the long-term incomes of producer members by attempting to overcome some of the inherent weaknesses of the farmers' position in the market. Metcalf suggests various methods which can be used to achieve this objective, and these will be considered now, with examples of how they have actually been used in practice by Boards in the United Kingdom.

The first major method of achieving the objective is to reduce on-farm production costs. This can be achieved in two ways, either by encouraging greater internal technical efficiency, or by bargaining with suppliers of necessary inputs. The United Kingdom Federation of Milk Marketing Boards, for example, have attempted to improve technical efficiency of production by the introduction of incentives, and latterly compulsion, to encourage farmers to instal bulk milk tanks on their farms. On their members' behalf, the Milk Marketing Boards undertook negotiations with manufacturers of bulk tanks with regard to price and specification.

The second major alternative available to Boards is to attempt to increase demand for their commodities. This can be done by controlling the quality of production, a technique used by all marketing boards, and also by the use of advertising. Marketing Boards have been major advertisers of their products in an attempt to stimulate demand. 'Drinka Pinta Milka Day' is now a well known household phrase. The questionable success of such generic advertising is discussed in Chapter 3. Boards can also attempt to find new outlets for their products. To again mention the Milk Marketing Boards, they were very active in the establishment of a British market for yoghurt, a milk-based product, and in encouraging the introduction of milk vending machines in as many locations as possible.

The third possibility open to Boards is to maximize, or at least improve, returns from a given demand for their commodity. This can be achieved using a variety of methods, principally:

(a) by the use of countervailing power to bargain with the initial buyers of their output;
(b) by the provision of market intelligence and research;
(c) by the encouragement of greater competition in the selling of the product. The Milk Marketing Boards, for example, operate retail outlets in their own rights;
(d) by direction of the distribution channels through which the product travels;
(e) by controlling the supply of the product. The Potato Marketing Board, for example, set an acreage quota which limits the output of their product; and
(f) by the use of price discrimination, charging prices which differ according to the end use of the product. The Milk Marketing Boards for example have different prices for milk for manufacturing and milk for liquid consumption.

In practice the most widespread controls used by Marketing Boards have covered the supply of their product, and the use of discriminatory pricing techniques. Both are the most suspect areas of success. It was quickly established that there is a direct correlation between the success of a Marketing Board for a commodity and the success of that Board in controlling the output of its members. Kimber (1977), for example, describes the outstanding success of the Guernsey Tomato Marketing Board in improving the returns of its producer members. This is achieved as a result of rigid controls over output, covering both quality and quantity.

3. *Success and failure of Boards in practice*

At various times there have been Boards in existence in the United Kingdom for commodities so diverse as milk, wool, potatoes, hops, pigs, tomatoes, cucumbers, and eggs. Each Board would seem to have enjoyed a differing degree of success, although it is difficult to establish what should constitute successful operation. This is because the Board does not fall into a simple classification of private enterprise, or government agency, but comprises a mixture of both.

Zif and Israeli (1978) identify five areas of relevance to the performance evaluation of marketing boards. These are profitability, productivity, market development, social responsibility, and innovation. These criteria can be used successfully in countries, principally developing ones, where monopoly export marketing boards have replaced firms which were formerly engaged in the export trade. Experience in the United Kingdom suggests, however, that marketing boards have been deemed successes or failures on much narrower grounds.

The continuing existence of marketing boards depends totally on producer satisfaction with the way in which they are operating. At any time producers can vote a Board out of existence, and have done in the case of the Tomato and Cucumber Board. The Minister of Agriculture also has the power to discontinue a Board, as was done in the case of the British Egg Marketing Board.

The operation of three Marketing Boards will now be considered in depth in order to show how Boards work in practice, and also to show why some Boards have operated more successfully than others in the United Kingdom.

The Milk Marketing Board. Before the First World War the marketing of milk was completely free. Throughout the war there were restrictions on imports, and government intervention encouraged the production and manufacturing of milk. Price controls continued until 1920 when imports were again made available. These consisted of cheap manufactured milk products, and as in addition home production exceeded demand, there was considerable pressure to reduce prices.

In 1922 the NFU set up a permanent Joint Milk Committee with the National Dairymens Association to agree milk prices for a year. This encouraged an increase in production and prices became even more depressed. The price for the year was agreed in September, and the system worked effectively until 1929 when many buyers did not appear in September to renew their contracts. Agreement was reached in October at a very low price.

Separate prices were, even at this time, paid for manufacturing milk and liquid milk and the 1930/31 contract was particularly unfavourable to farmers since it gave the buyer the option to choose under which category he would buy the milk. In addition these contract terms were applicable only to certain buying areas, of which London was the most important and although a contract was binding on producers and buyers once it had been finalized, there was no compulsion to make such a contract. There was also considerable opportunity for evasion of the contracts.

As contract terms grew harsher with the virtual collapse of the international market, the situation became more and more chaotic, and by the end of the period the machinery of the Joint Milk Committee became almost wholly ineffective. The only real weapon which producers possessed was to withhold supplies from the liquid market, however, with so many small producers on the verge of bankruptcy any concerted action in that direction was highly improbable.

There was thus an obvious need, from the viewpoint of the producer, for large-scale organization of the production and marketing of milk in the United Kingdom. This was provided in 1932 when plans were laid before Parliament for a compulsory Marketing Board for milk. In 1933, when dairy farmers were given the opportunity to vote on the plans, 89 per cent of registered producers, responsible for 96 per cent of cows, voted in favour of a marketing scheme. The Milk Marketing Board has been in existence since that date.

There are, in fact, five Marketing Boards in operation. These are run separately mainly because of transportation problems associated with liquid milk. All five Boards do, however, work in very close association. In 1933 a Board covering producers in England and Wales was introduced, and a Board for producers in the South of Scotland, known as the Scottish Milk Marketing Board. In 1934 the North of Scotland Board, and the Aberdeen and District Board were both established. Finally, in 1935, the Milk Marketing Board for Northern Ireland was set up.

The number of members of the five Boards is very varied. Table 7.1 shows the numbers of registered milk producers in each Board area in 1979. It should be noted that the Boards have varying registration requirements. Table 7.1 does, however, give a good indication of the number of producers in each area.

Table 7.1. Number of registered milk producers,
by Board area, in 1979

Board	Number of producers
England and Wales	46 972
Scottish	3117
Aberdeen and District	228
North of Scotland	155
Northern Ireland	10 336
Total	60 808

Source: M.M.B. (1979).

The control of the Boards is in the hands of producers. The England and Wales Board, for example, has an executive of 18 members; 12 of whom are elected regionally, three nationally, and three are nominated by the Minister of Agriculture.

There are in addition regional committees which make recommendations to the national committee. It is very much a producer's organization, and the Milk Marketing Boards like to be seen as statutorily organized co-operatives. The controls exerted stem from the requirement that all producers must be registered with the Milk Marketing Board, who are the sole buyers of milk. A licence must be obtained if sales are to be made direct from the farm.

There is a guaranteed market for all milk produced by members; this is sold on the producer's behalf by the Board. One price is paid for all milk, regardless of the place of production, or the end use of the milk, and perhaps most importantly the milk is paid for at the same time every month. Payment is by cheque directly into the account of the producer.

The penalty for selling milk without a licence, to anyone other than the Board, is a punitive fine. The basis of the organizational success of the Milk Marketing Board is tied closely to discipline.

The price of milk varies seasonally to encourage a balanced production of milk throughout the year. Without this there would be a tendency for much higher production during the summer months. There is also a certain regional fluctuation in the price of milk, in an attempt to balance the different transport costs of the regions. Obviously the more remote regions have disproportionately high transport costs. The base price of milk for the year is agreed by the

EEC Council of Ministers at their annual review of prices. The prices actually paid to producers are calculated from the base price.

There are three major outlets for milk sales off the farm: sales made wholesale to distributors and manufacturers, some producers retail their milk direct to the customers, and some milk is held on the farm for farmhouse cheesemaking. Wholesale outlets are of dominant importance at the present time.

In 1979, 51 per cent of milk produced in the United Kingdom was sold on the liquid market, with the remainder being used for various manufactured products, cream, cheese, butter, milk puddings, chocolate crumb and so on. In the outlying production areas such as Devon and Cornwall and South Wales the majority of the milk produced is processed into higher value, lower bulk products. This is a source of some discontent among producers located near to the major cities. A number of farmers have complained about having to subsidize the remotely located farmers who receive virtually the same price for a product in less demand in their locality than on the periphery of major population centres.

The Milk Marketing Board acts as agent for its producer members and obtains different prices for the milk which it sells to different outlets. Production is split into two markets, liquid and manufacturing, and the Board acts as a discriminating monopolist, there being separate prices for each market. As much milk as possible is sold on the liquid market, where prices are highest. Liquid milk prices are set by Government edict. Any milk not required for liquid consumption is sold for manufacturing at whatever price is available on the market. In 1977-8 the average price paid for milk for manufacturing was 41 per cent of the average retail price.

When the Board was set up it initially set the retail price for milk. During the Second World War the War Agricultural Executive Committee took over this function, and since then the Government has set the retail price, through the Ministry of Agriculture. The Government also traditionally set the base price which the producer received for his output, until this function was taken over by the EEC Agricultural Commission.

The price which the producer receives for his output is subject to a number of premia and deductions. Basic prices are set regionally, reflecting to a certain extent varying levels of demand for liquid milk. The basic price also varies seasonally in an attempt to reduce fluctuations in levels of supply throughout the year. Premia are available for milk supplied through bulk tanks, and the higher the quality of the milk measured in terms of butter fat and solids non-fat, the higher the price paid to the farmer. Deductions are made to cover the capital costs of maintaining the structure of the Board, and the Board collects, on behalf of the EEC, the co-responsibility levy which is charged on dairy producers.

The Milk Marketing Boards provide a number of ancillary services. Any producers making use of them can charge the cost against the monthly milk cheque. The most important service provided is that of Artificial Insemination (AI), the aim of which is to improve the quality and quantity of milk production in the UK through the genetic improvement of dairy cattle.

Another service provided by the Milk Marketing Board is the National Milk Recording Scheme which was also designed to improve the yields of dairy cows. By recording the yields of individual cows it is possible to eliminate the poor yielders, and acquire information to improve breeding programmes. The Board's Farm Management Service extends beyond the bounds of dairy production, covering the total farm business and again reflects a desire for more efficient production and management. Overall the emphasis is very firmly on the interrelationship of the production and marketing of dairy production, in that the marketing efficiency of the Board can be significantly improved by increased production efficiency at the farm level.

The operations of the Milk Marketing Board were placed under close analysis following the accession of the United Kingdom to full membership of the EEC. At one time it seemed highly unlikely that the Board would be able to continue in its present form, because it operated in direct contravention to the spirit of CAP. Eventually, however, agreement was reached that Marketing Boards for milk should be permissible in the UK, and in any other EEC member country, so long as certain preconditions were met. Authorization had first to be gained from producers of the commodity, along the lines previously indicated. In 1979 UK milk producers voted to indicate whether or not they wished their Board to continue, and the result was an overwhelming vote of confidence in favour of the Board. Over 99 per cent of producers voted in favour of the continuance of the existing arrangements.

In addition to producers being in favour of a Board being set up, the percentage of milk used for direct human consumption, as liquid milk or fresh products, in the member country concerned must be at least one and a half times greater than the corresponding percentage for the Community as a whole, while consumption per capita must be greater than the Community average.

Provided these conditions are met a Marketing Board can be granted the exclusive right to purchase all milk from its producers. This is subject to certain exceptions, such as the right for producers to retail their output direct to the consumer. With this right goes the obligation to buy and market all milk, of suitable quality, that is offered. All returns from the market can be pooled and equalized prices paid to producers, regardless of the use to which the individual producers milk is put.

At the behest of one per cent of producers a referendum may be held at any time to determine whether the Board continues to hold the support of its members, except that there must be at least a 5 year gap between ballots. Where the required number of votes in favour is not received, the Commission is empowered to withdraw the authorization of that Board.

As a result, the marketing of milk in the United Kingdom continues to be organized in much the same way as it has been for the last 40 years. The problems which remain, and which affect all milk producers, result mainly from the EEC structural imbalances and overproduction, even though the United Kingdom is, itself, not self-sufficient for milk and dairy products.

The Potato Marketing Board. The Potato Marketing Board was one of the first Boards to be established in 1934. It was suspended for the duration of the Second World War and for a period afterwards but was then resumed in 1955 under the Potato Marketing Scheme, giving it powers of regulating production, and the right to implement the Government guarantee to potato producers.

The Potato Marketing Board, unlike the Milk Marketing Board, has relied mainly on controls over production to realize its aims. Four main controls are utilized by the Board:

1. Producers of 0.5 ha or more cannot sell their potatoes unless they are registered with the Potato Marketing Board. The producer pays a levy to the Board per hectare planted. Producers are allocated production quotas, and producing more than the quota incurs a levy per excess hectare grown.

2. The Board can make prescriptive resolutions having the force of law. In addition to acreage regulations, it also enforced upper riddle sizes up to 1969.
3. Growers commonly sell through merchants licensed by the Board, although they can obtain licences to be grower salesmen, and then make farmgate sales.
4. In years of excess supply the Board purchases surplus potatoes. These are sprayed with potato dye to indicate that they are not for human consumption and are then sold back to farmers for feeding to stock.

From 1955 to 1959 there was an individual guarantee to each farmer which encouraged maximum production without any concern for quality. From 1959 on there has been a guarantee for the whole crop. Any difference between the guaranteed price and the average price realized over the year is made up by the Potato Marketing Board.

In years of surplus production Board control is by acreage control and surplus buying. There is a Government payment of £2 for every £1 the Board pays towards surplus buying. Most of the Potato Marketing Board's guarantee money is used in support buying.

The quota which the Potato Marketing Board allows is related to the last 3 years' acreage of the producer. The producer is allowed to grow a standard percentage of the average of his acreages grown in the previous three years, this percentage being set in August and related to growing conditions and forecasted grower intentions. There are health restrictions covering the import of potatoes. Prior to full membership of the EEC there was a complete ban on the import of main crop potatoes, except during times of shortage. Potatoes for processing faced an import duty of 15 per cent. Transport costs also increased the price of imports, potatoes generally have a low value in relation to weight. They are easily damaged in transport, and have a fairly short life.

The major difficulties faced by the Potato Marketing Board result from the problem of achieving level supplies because of the immense variations in yields according to the weather. Yields can vary to a very great extent from year to year, and potatoes cannot be stored from one year to the next. The wild fluctuations in supply also occur in conditions of extremely inelastic demand. The only thing which changes demand significantly is when prices increase to a large extent, as in 1976 and 1977, and following such a period, demand is very slow to respond to a reduction in prices.

As a result of full EEC membership the status of the Potato Marketing Board was called into question, in particular the control which it exercised over imports of main crop potatoes. In 1979 the preclusion of imports was found to be illegal by the European Court, and since that time free trade has been allowed for potatoes. Because of market conditions it is unlikely that home production will ever be threatened by cheap imports, however, freak returns for producers as a result of poor growing conditions are unlikely ever to occur again.

The Potato Marketing Board continues to operate in the free market and each year sets a guaranteed price. This is the price which the Board would pay for potatoes offered to it by producers. The Board is empowered to place up to 500 000 tonnes of potatoes under contract each year, and by this means endeavours to improve market stability. Each registered producer is allowed to offer to the Board up to 12½ per cent of his output of potatoes, and is allowed to indicate to the Board preferred periods of delivery between November and May inclusive.

The Potato Marketing Board has been subject to periodic revolts amongst its members. In 1965 one producer went to prison rather than pay his dues. The Board is undoubtedly only mildly efficient in marketing the produce of its members. It has involved itself mainly with production technology, at the expense of any major involvement in the marketing of the commodity. It is difficult, however, to suggest any alternative method of supporting production which would prove more efficient. Without controls there would be chaos in the market. The efficient producer, as always, would survive, although overall there would almost certainly be a reduction in production efficiency, and a return to pre-1930s conditions.

The British Egg Marketing Board. The British Egg Marketing Board is a classic example of what can go wrong with a Marketing Board. It illustrates very well the difficulties which confront any efforts to control the supply of a commodity which is in universal demand by any method, other than the crude operation of supply and demand on the price level.

The British Egg Marketing Board was second in size and importance to the Milk Marketing Board, and was set up in 1956. The first and most urgent task of the Board was to deal with overproduction. When it came into being British producers had already acquired 95 per cent of the home market for shell eggs, consumption was relatively high, and although there was still scope for expansion of the British share of the manufacturing market, this was a very small section of the total market. Also in 1956 the production of eggs had been transformed into a highly technically efficient process. Production conditions were therefore very different from those of other commodities where marketing boards had been introduced successfully.

During the Second World War and in the years afterwards the Government had kept control of egg marketing and had set up a network of packing stations throughout Britain. In 1956 control was handed back to the industry, and it was felt that some central authority was needed to take over the administration of egg marketing, handling subsidies, organization of packing stations and so on. However, there was far from universal acceptance that a marketing board would be the most suitable means of achieving this, and the British Egg Marketing Board only came into being after 34 days of public enquiry during which 1040 objections to the scheme were lodged, and as a result the powers of the Board were modified considerably from those originally proposed.

The great weakness of the British Egg Marketing Board was that, whereas the Milk Marketing Board has complete 'horizontal' control, since all the home-produced milk is channelled through it, the British Egg Marketing Board had to accept all eggs offered to it but had no powers to prevent farmers dealing direct with consumers. So on 1 July 1957, when the British Egg Marketing Board began its operations, it was in the unsatisfactory situation of facing overproduction with considerably restricted powers.

The most crucial misjudgement made by the Board was introduced within the first few weeks of its existence, and it was a mistake from which the British Egg Marketing Board never recovered. Eggs passing through a packing station were stamped, primarily to prevent the Government subsidy being paid twice. Although the lion stamp was intended to carry a connotation of freshness it quickly became associated, not with quality, but with lack of it. As a measure of public preference, it was estimated that by 1968 as much as 40 per cent of total British egg production bypassed the Board and was sold direct to the retailer, or through farm-gate sales to the consumer. These eggs did not qualify for subsidy, however, neither did they contribute to the expenses of the Board, which were determined by the amounts of eggs which it handled. Also in periods of glut, farmers selling the bulk of their eggs direct were completely free to offload any surplus to the packing stations. This added to the difficulties of the Board, and detracted considerably from its strength.

The Board was charged at its inception with four functions. The first was to organize the collection and distribution of eggs offered to it by producers. This it achieved reasonably efficiently through a network of 500 packing stations situated throughout Britain. The second function was to distribute the Government subsidy on egg production. This was a very complex system organized to the satisfaction of the industry. The third function was to stimulate demand for eggs. Although the Board had a very high advertising budget, the effect which this had on demand was questionable.

The fourth function of the Board was to control the supply of eggs. This was the area of greatest failure for the British Egg Marketing Board. The Board proved to be a totally unsuitable vehicle for the control of output, mainly because it lacked the power to channel all production through its own outlets.

Over time the industry built up a fierce opposition to the operation of the Board, and organized itself to oppose it. In 1968 the British Egg Association, a fierce critic of Board policy, combined with all the major poultry organizations to form a Federation of British Poultry directly opposed to the British Egg Marketing Board. In response to this opposition the Government set up a Commission of Inquiry which reported in May 1968. The most important recommendations were, firstly, that the Board should be discontinued; secondly, that the subsidy should be abolished after a suitable transition period; thirdly, that egg stamping should not be obligatory; fourthly, that seconds should be allowed back on the market, and finally, that a small central authority should be set up with responsibility for a general oversight of the interests of the industry.

The powers of this central authority should include support buying of seasonal surpluses or in emergency, the provision of market intelligence and research, quality control, and limited national advertising, to be paid for by a levy on all producers.

The British Egg Marketing Board responded with a circular to all producers asking for their support, however, it failed to influence the Government's decision. The report was accepted almost *in toto*, the Board was discontinued over a period, and the Eggs Authority formed. This took over from the Board in the early part of 1971.

The Eggs Authority undertakes the work proposed for it by the Committee of Inquiry, and its functions are controlled by 13 members. There are four independent members, four members appointed after consultation with trade organizations to represent the interests of egg packers, distributors, retailers, wholesalers, food manufacturers, and ancillary trades to egg production, such as rearing and hatching, and five members appointed after consultation with producer organizations, such as Goldenlay.

In conclusion it is only fair to note that producer dissatisfaction is now occasionally vented on the functions of the Eggs Authority. Competition within the industry is fierce, and returns as a result often marginal. There is considerable resentment about the levy payable to the Eggs Authority by all producers, although the work which it carries out probably benefits every participant in the industry. The most obvious work carried out is the extensive advertising programme. There are also numerous other aspects of its functions.

4. *Summary*

The foregoing consideration of the operation of three of the Marketing Boards which have operated, and still operate, in this country highlight the dependence of Boards on the supply and demand characteristics of the industry for their success or failure. Control is probably the most crucial factor here. The three Boards which have proved most successful over time, those for milk, hops, and wool, exercise some control over the output of their members, and can, in consequence, organize the marketing of the produce which they handle very efficiently. The less successful Boards, notably those for tomatoes and cucumbers, pigs, and eggs lacked the necessary control over their members. The Tomato and Cucumber Board, for example, did not assume compulsory powers, and quickly fell foul of the wrath of disillusioned producer members.

This central problem, of sufficient and efficient control, is something which has hampered the successful development of voluntary marketing co-operatives in this country over the years, as will be illustrated in the next chapter.

One of the aims of the Marketing Boards has always been to impress upon members the requirements of the market, and in so doing help members to improve the quality, presentation, and marketing of their products. To this extent they have achieved very little success, farmers still tend to be concerned chiefly with aspects of production, and this is probably due to a combination of factors:

1. In certain cases farmers regard Boards simply as instruments of price negotiation and not at all as an instrument for the improvement of their own productive and marketing techniques.
2. Overall agricultural policy in this country has not encouraged farmers to be anything other than production orientated.
3. Because of their size and anonymity, it is very difficult for the Boards to communicate with their members, making large scale changes in the refinements of their output highly unlikely.
4. Boards have been loathe to upset member goodwill by heavy handed use of available compulsory powers.

In considering the continuing role of Marketing Boards as vehicles for the efficient disposal of agricultural output, it is probably fair to say that their most important role lies in an international context. In the United Kingdom the heyday of the Marketing Board is past, as a result of changing political and technological circumstances, and the introduction of alternative methods of farm income support. However, having said that, the removal of the existing Marketing Boards in the UK, particularly those covering milk, would undoubtedly have a deleterious effect upon the efficiency of the marketing of the commodities covered by Boards.

8. Voluntary producer co-operation

Co-operation in agriculture

Statutory marketing organizations do not provide the only examples of farmers' co-operation. There is a long tradition of farmers joining together in some parts of their business in cases where there is no legal compulsion upon them to do so. This is the essence of voluntary co-operation, and in recent years such a collaboration has been viewed by many as the farmer's major hope of improving his returns from the market.

A co-operative has been defined by the Central Council for Agricultural and Horticultural Cooperation as an association of producers who together can achieve some commercial objective more successfully than they can as individuals. The commercial objective is usually to make more profit than could be achieved if the farmer operated as an individual in the market. A similar definition is given by the International Labour Organization which describes a formal co-operative as 'an association of persons which has recognised the similarity of certain of their needs and the possibility of satisfying these better through a common undertaking than by individual means'. Again the emphasis is placed on the commercial aims of the association.

The major objective of co-operatives can be summarized as aiming to provide a continuing, independent force, strong enough to exert an influence on the market, for the benefit of, and within the control of, its trading members. From this it can be seen that the co-operative aims to provide continuity, independence, and strength, through the maintenance of a market share for its members, operating at all times at a profit. This is very different from the non-profit oriented approach of the early co-operative movement.

Co-operatives have always aimed to reward members in proportion to the amount of trading which they channel through the association. This is summarized by Morley (1975) who suggests that societies must conduct their businesses so as to show that their main business is the mutual benefit of their members, and that the benefits enjoyed by a member depends upon the use he makes of the facilities provided by the co-operative and not upon the amount of money invested by the member in the society.

There are ten major principles underlying the co-operatives which operate in British agriculture. These can be summarized as follows:

1. The co-operative takes the form of an incorporated society, or company, registered under one of the following Acts: the Partnership Act of 1890, the Companies Acts of 1948 and 1967, or the Industrial and Provident Societies Acts of 1965 and 1968. For production and service groups, partnership agreements are probably best. If registration is made under the Companies Acts then a minimum of two members is required, for the Industrial and Provident Societies Act the minimum is seven members. Limited liability is obtained if registration is via the Companies or the Industrial and Provident Societies Acts.
2. By law at least 90 per cent of shareholders must be producers.
3. All members have equal rights.
4. Control of shares lies in the hands of directors.
5. There is a principle of one man, one vote, regardless of the size of holding in the co-operative.
6. Profits are regarded as a surplus after taking into account provisions for taxation and reinvestment, and are distributed as a bonus on trade to members.
7. Interest on share and loan capital is limited to 2 per cent over Bank of England base rate or 7 per cent, whichever is higher. Shares are valued at par.
8. Shareholding is limited, with a maximum individual holding of £5000.
9. Non-member trade must not exceed one third of total turnover.
10. The co-operative is entirely within the control of its membership.

The history of co-operation in the United Kingdom

There is a long tradition of co-operation in agriculture extending back for over 100 years. In 1867 the first Agricultural and Horticultural Association was established in Manchester by Greening, one of the original Rochdale Pioneers, providing fertilizers and feeding stuffs of guaranteed quality. This survived for 50 years, having been stimulated by the then regular fraud of supplying sub-standard products. It was patterned in style of the consumer co-operatives.

In 1901 the British Agricultural Organization Society (AOS) was formed, patterned on the Irish AOS, its terms of references including securing the co-operation of all connected with the land. By 1902, 22 requisite societies existed; along with 11 milk co-operatives and six co-operative banks. Before 1909 any co-operatives relied on voluntary income, but after this time the Board of Agriculture contributed £1200 to promote co-operation amongst smallholders.

During the First World War there was a considerable amount of amalgamation, forming county organizations such as West Cumberland Farmers. The Government grant was changed to be on a pound to pound basis depending on the amount the farmers themselves put in. By the end of the war the size of the co-operative movement was large enough to be of consequence. During the latter war years the consumer movement allied itself to the Labour Party, breaking a basic co-operative principle. This clashed with many farming interests, and supplemented the fall of the co-operatives in the 1920s. In 1918 the Agricultural Wholesale Society Ltd. was formed to operate as a buying agency for agricultural crops.

In 1920 the depression began, lasting through the 1920s, reducing the contributions which the AOS received, and thus also reducing Government support. In 1924 the Agricultural Wholesale Society collapsed. This led to a sharp fall in the prestige of co-operation, and the collapse of the AOS in the same year. During the 1930s the NFU took over the advisory role of co-operatives. There was further depression in agriculture, and it was decided to form Marketing Boards, wiping out much of the need for co-operatives. At the same time the requisite societies gained strength, there being numerous amalgamations.

By 1936 there was a semblance of an apex organization starting up, with the formation of the Agricultural Co-operatives Managers Association, formed to provide liaison between the individual co-operatives and the NFU. In 1945 the co-operatives and the NFU sponsored the formation of the Agricultural Co-operative Association (ACA), similar to the AOS. In 1955 the Fatstock Marketing Corporation was formed, following the failure to establish a

Livestock Marketing Board, and a Farmers Central Organization (FCO) was formed to try to co-ordinate NFU business activities.

In 1956 the Agricultural Central Co-operative Association (ACCA) was formed, with the backing of the NFU, amalgamating the ACA and the FCO. Its duties included providing legal advice to co-operatives, Parliamentary lobbying, and providing efficiency studies. One of the ACCA successes was in gaining Agricultural Co-operatives exemption from the terms of the Restrictive Trades Practices Act. In 1961 Agricultural Central Trading Ltd., a national requisite group, was established.

In 1962 the Government set up a body known as the Agricultural Marketing and Development Committee (AMDEC) with a budget of £2.5 million to be spent over 3 years on investigating marketing efficiency and estimating the success of paid producer co-operatives. This stimulated the formation of small scale co-operatives normally known as groups.

In 1966 the Agricultural Central Co-operative Association broke down, and an Agricultural Co-operative Association was formed, representing a break with the National Farmers Union. In 1967 the Agriculture Act made available £40 millions to be spent over 5 years for the purposes of co-operation. A new body known as the Central Council for Agricultural and Horticultural Co-operation took over the functions of AMDEC. In the first years of its operation the Central Council gave grants on the working capital of co-operatives in the first few years of their operation. In 1971, however, the political mood changed, AMDEC was wound up, and the Central Council could no longer make grants on working capital.

In 1972 the NFU and ACA amalgamated again to form Agricultural Co-operation and Marketing Services Ltd. (ACMS) providing legal and other advice to farmers forming co-operatives, and sending representatives to COGECA, the General Committee of Agricultural Co-operation in the EEC.

When the Central Council for Agricultural and Horticultural Co-operation was formed it was charged with three main functions. These are:

(i)   to organize, promote, encourage, develop and co-ordinate co-operation in agriculture and horticulture;
(ii) to advise Ministers on all matters relating to co-operation in agriculture and horticulture; and

(iii) to administer a scheme of grants chiefly designed to aid co-operative activities in production and marketing.

In 1974 the Central Council was given the additional responsibility of setting up a Marketing Unit to assist the development of marketing co-operatives in the United Kingdom. This is guided by the Marketing Policy Committee. The Council has 14 members, appointed by the Ministers responsible for agricultural development in the United Kingdom. Six are independent members and eight are appointed from nominations made by the three Farmers Unions and the four General Co-operative Associations.

The Central Council has become the major administrative organization with regard to co-operation, and administers the available grants, initially provided by the United Kingdom government, and latterly by FEOGA, the European Agricultural Guidance and Guarantee Fund. The activities of the Central Council are very varied and fall into two major categories, advice and information, and grant aid and loan guarantees.

Whenever a project or scheme of any reasonable size is envisaged by a group of farmers it will almost certainly be worth their while to undertake a study of its feasibility. Such a study will investigate the existing situation of the producers, setting out the problems of the proposed system, and the extent to which it is likely to be successful. The administration of the project will be analysed, in particular the management, and also the financing of the scheme, should it come into operation.

The effects of the scheme on the individual members of the group will also be detailed, so that all members will be fully aware of the consequences of co-operation before they enter into any commitment. Some form of feasibility study is essential for any proposed venture, however small, and can make the difference between financial success and disaster.

The range of grants available to co-operatives is extensive, and includes a contribution towards the cost of feasibility studies. The formation costs of new co-operatives are subsidized, as are the costs of buildings and certain equipment. Finance is also available to aid managerial selection and training, and research costs are heavily subsidized. Each scheme is assessed on its merits, and as a result the rate of grant awarded varies.

Throughout the 1970s there has been a degree of confusion between the Central Council and ACMS over the development of co-operatives. The major role of ACMS was seen as that of representing the interests of co-operatives, particularly in Europe. However, it also sought to undertake a development function, similar to that of the Central Council. As a result of dissatisfaction in the success of ACMS in 1979 the NFU withdrew its contribution to ACMS; previously it contributed about one third of total income. ACMS continue to provide a representational function for co-operatives, and the NFU has set up a Marketing Development Committee to encourage the development of marketing at the individual farmer and co-operative level.

At the present time the influence of co-operatives on the marketing of all types of agricultural produce is considerable. Table 8.1 shows the estimated co-operative share of various markets in recent marketing years.

Table 8.1. Co-operative market shares for specified agricultural products in recent marketing years

	Percentage	Marketing year
Cereals	15.0	1977-78
Glasshouse vegetables	19.0	1976
Potatoes*	10.9	1976
Oil seed rape	40.0	1978-79
Top fruit	38.0	1976
Livestock	8.0	1975
Wool	39.5	1978-79
Eggs	29.1	1978

Source Central Council for Agricultural and Horticultural Co-operation statistics. I am indebted to Mr John Morley, of CCAHC, for the provision of a combination of published and unpublished information which has been used in compiling this table.
*Including seed potatoes

Although these figures show the extent of the development of co-operation in the United Kingdom, the market shares obtained are considerably less than those commanded by agricultural co-operatives throughout the rest of Europe. There are various reasons for this.

Agricultural co-operation in Europe

The majority of European countries produce in excess of domestic requirements for many commodities. This means that there is an exportable surplus and the consumer can afford to be more discriminating. To be competitive in export markets there is a requirement of standardization, and scale economies in the assembly process have been made. Also much greater use of market information services has been made than in the United Kingdom. Such standardization is made more feasible by co-operation among producers, and has occurred in Europe, accentuated by the serious problem of too many and too small farms.

The problems facing European producers were increased by the absence of any marketing boards or price guarantees. Instead, governmental assistance tended to be given to encourage the formation of co-operatives. In the Netherlands, for example, horticultural products must be sold by auction, and all the auctions are owned by co-operatives. In Norway, the 1930 Marketing Act placed a levy on all agricultural producers and only co-operatives could benefit from the funds so generated.

Another reason why co-operatives have traditionally been of greater importance in the rest of Europe than in the UK is related to the existence of reasonably well-developed banking interests in the UK at the time of the Agricultural Revolution. Farmers who were intensifying their production, as a result of the new techniques which were being made available, were able, therefore, to borrow money from established sources of finance. On the Continent, such facilities did not exist in the nineteenth century and special credit institutions had to be generated within agriculture. Credit co-operatives were set up, inviting deposits from anyone, and investing their capital in agricultural co-operatives. These bodies still exist today and offer considerable financial benefits to their farmer members.

In 1967 a set of EEC rules was produced regarding aids which member states are permitted to give to stimulate co-operation among farmers. These are very substantial, including, for example, a capital grant of 50 per cent for up to 3 years after the formation of a new co-operative, and loans towards building and machinery costs of up to 40 per cent in the first 5 years of operation. To qualify for such aids, farmers have to guarantee to sell all their produce through co-operatives.

Despite the fact that the United Kingdom is now a full member of the EEC, there is still much less use made of co-operation in the UK than in the rest of the EEC. An EEC Commission Report (1977) suggests that this is partly due to the fact that co-operatives in the UK are unattractive to investors because of the tax structure and legal system.

United Kingdom co-operatives are limited in the level of interest they can pay on investments; shares cannot increase in equity value to be used as a hedge against inflation; they are not marketable in the same way as quoted company shares and they cannot be sold for more than their face value—all of which, it is claimed, keeps investment down.

The other major problem facing co-operatives in the United Kingdom is that although shares are not marketable they can be 'cashed in', often at short notice or on demand. This can weaken the co-operative's finances just at a time when their demand for capital is expanding.

If co-operatives are to improve the inward flow of cash they must be attractive to outside lenders. However, more external cash would mean a further dilution of farmer members' independence and would also require changes in the fiscal and legal frameworks to maintain the balance between the membership and the sources of external finance.

A considerable contrast is seen in the case of Denmark, a country which entered the EEC at the same time as the United Kingdom. In Denmark not only is there a greater will among farmers to co-operate, but the taxation and legal systems encourage it. Although Danish farmers have to pay income tax and corporation tax if the co-operative makes a profit, as in the UK, the level is considerably lower than that levied on a limited liability company. In the UK the level is the same. Also the legal guidelines on what constitutes a co-operative are less constricting in Denmark than in the UK.

Agricultural marketing in Denmark is dominated by co-operatives; 90 per cent of slaughter pigs and milk, for example, and 40 per cent of slaughter cattle and eggs are handled by co-operatives. On the input side an increasing proportion of the fertilizer and feeding-stuffs trade and farm machinery are purchased through co-operatives.

It is possible, of course, that in future the importance of co-operatives in the United Kingdom will increase. Consideration of future circumstances will be given at the close of this chapter, however, prior to that, a review will be made of the most important forms of co-operation used by farmers in the United Kingdom.

Types of co-operation

There are various types of co-operation available to farmers, varying in complexity, and in the degree of loyalty required of their members. Five major types of co-operation can be identified, namely machinery sharing; production co-operation, marketing co-operation, co-operation in the supply of farmer's requisites, and federal co-operation. These will now be considered in turn.

1. *Machinery sharing*

Many farmers in the United Kingdom have found it worth their while, in certain circumstances, to share many kinds of farm machinery and equipment. This enables the farm to take advantage of up-to-date, efficient, and labour saving equipment at less than the cost which would be required if the purchase was made independently. Such machines would often not be justified economically for an independent purchase.

There are various advantages resulting from machinery sharing which can be summarized as follows:

(i)   a reduction in capital investment requirements for machinery per acre;
(ii) fuller use and availability of high capacity machinery resulting in reduced running costs per acre;
(iii) manpower from each farm can be pooled, if required, to make up a more efficient team at peak periods;
(iv) money saved as a result of the reduced capital investment can be put to other uses.

Machinery sharing may take one of two forms, being either informal or formal. Informal sharing is of very great significance in the UK. Virtually every farmer shares one or more pieces of machinery with a neighbour, or some member of his family. It is an aspect of co-operation whose importance is often underrated. It works very well at a personal level; problems can arise, however, if partners wish to use the machinery at the same time.

Formal sharing attempts to overcome this problem by drawing up a set of rules to ensure control, cover maintenance responsibility for the machines, insurance, rota for use, and so on. For farmers who enter into formal machinery-sharing agreements there are four main sources of finance available. The first is bank borrowing which is often the cheapest form of credit, so long as the farmers co-operating have a reasonable working relationship with the bank manager. Banks are becoming increasingly interested in lending money to cover the purchase of machinery, as the costs of machines, particularly harvesting equipment, have increased. All the major banks now have schemes designed to facilitate the purchase of machinery and these can be taken advantage of by groups of farmers as well as by individuals. A second source of finance is available through hire purchase. This, however, is the most expensive form of credit, and should only be entered into if all other forms of capital are unobtainable.

As a third alternative leasing of the machinery can be considered under some formal agreement with a credit company or a machinery manufacturer. Leasing is of increasing importance in United Kingdom agriculture and offers a number of advantages in a machinery sharing situation.

The final possibility for obtaining finance is through the use of Syndicate Credit Companies. The Second World War had accentuated the development of farm machinery, and gave the first opportunity for machinery sharing. This was formalized in the south of England in the 1950s and led to the formation of various County Syndicate Credit Companies, usually administered by the County NFU secretary. Any group of two or more farmers who purchase a mobile machine together can borrow up to 80 per cent of the purchase price of the machine from their County Syndicate Credit Company. This is repayable in half yearly instalments at Bank of England Minimum Lending Rate plus 2 per cent, on a diminishing balance over a period of 4 years. The most important factor in this form of borrowing is that interest is paid on the reducing balance of money owed, not on the initial sum loaned.

There are considerable opportunities available for machinery sharing, although there is far from universal acceptance of the principles involved. The major factor mediating against it is the loss of independence which is required. Also the work schedule of the farm is limited to the availability of the machine, and this can occasionally be very inconvenient.

2. *Production co-operation*

Production co-operation is an extension of the principle of machinery syndication, requiring a greater degree of commitment from farmer members. Not only is the machinery shared in a production co-operative, but in addition labour is pooled, along prearranged lines, to operate the production process in unison.

Co-operatives of this nature have been introduced for various aspects of production, particularly the making of winter fodder and the production of livestock. The machinery required for making winter fodder is both very expensive and labour intensive. It also has a very limited seasonal useage. These factors have combined to produce, in many cases, a situation where neighbouring farmers have found it to be in their mutual interest to make their winter fodder via a co-operative venture.

The reasoning behind livestock production co-operatives is rather different, although the rationale, to improve the efficiency of production, is the same. Many breeders of beef cattle who do not have a lot of breeding cows could benefit financially from working closely with other farmers who have similar enterprises. This also applies to sheep breeders, and mixed grazing of many types of land by cattle and by sheep, together or one after the other in rotation, can be beneficial both to the stock and to the grass.

This does not necessarily entail joint ownership of the animal involved. There will be advantages from the system even if individual ownership is maintained. However, the co-operating farmers may decide to buy jointly top quality bulls or rams, and even some top quality heifers or ewes, which individually they might not have been able to afford or justify.

Production co-operatives work successfully so long as they are entered into carefully. Substantial proportions of the farm are likely to be committed to co-operative management and utilization, and such an arrangement should not be entered into lightly.

There are various guidelines for consideration which can contribute to the success of a production co-operative. One is a compatible membership, taking into account the number of partners, their locations, the sizes of the farms and the systems of farming; a second is a sound organizational structure, possibly encompassed in a partnership agreement, with a record kept of decisions made, and with administration and finance agreed by all members of the co-operative; and a third is a soundly formulated policy, identifying the goals of the co-operative, and standardizing the systems of operation.

3. *Marketing co-operation*

In marketing co-operation, farmers join together to market, as one, part, or all, of the produce of their holdings. The theoretical basis for such co-operation is related to three major factors:

1. Bargaining power: increasing the bargaining strength of the farmer, which is weak and disorganized in relation to buyers.
2. Market economies: reducing the costs of marketing, by improving the efficiency of existing services, or achieving scale economies in certain operations.
3. Market investment: providing an additional investment opportunity so that the marketing of the commodity or commodities covered by the co-operative is considered as an additional enterprise to those already carried out by the farmer.

Each of these is associated to some extent with size of operation, and they are interrelated one with another. So, for example, to improve their bargaining strength, a group of farmers might join together in selling their produce, but to achieve any real bargaining power they will probably have to undertake some market service, such as assembly or grading. This in turn offers possibilities of scale economies, which may yield a financial reward irrespective of a bargaining advantage.

Furthermore, if the project involves capital expenditure, for example to provide a storage shed, this might be considered as a new enterprise in its own right, with its own associated returns. Similarly with increased size, members will be better informed of market conditions, improving their bargaining position in relation to market opponents.

Until recently, there have been very few instances of successful marketing co-operatives in the United Kingdom. There were many attempts at co-operation, and the general failure has been associated with a number of factors. One was the generally low standard of management of marketing co-operatives, brought about by the reluctance of farmers to pay high enough salaries to attract able men. Another major factor was the traditional constitution of co-operatives, making membership open to all comers. The major market advantage of a selling co-operative lies in its ability to enter into a contract for the supply of large quantities of a commodity in specified grades. This ability relies, in turn, on the willingness of farmers to enter into, and honour, contracts with their co-operative. However, in practice farmers have not exercised the necessary degree of market discipline. There have been numerous examples of farmers entering into contracts with a co-operative and then breaking them because the open market has temporarily offered a better return. The result is that co-operatives have been unable to offer a sufficient incentive to persuade farmers to sell together, rather than to independent traders.

The recent successes of marketing co-operation among farmers have stemmed from the introduction of what are known as producer groups. The groups share with the co-operative movement the basic principle of strength through unity, however, they differ in having restricted membership, so that farmers who deliberately fail to fulfil contracts may be excluded. Because of this they are not tied to the standards and welfare of the least efficient.

Agricultural marketing groups are a direct application of the theory or horizontal integration which involves bringing together units of production involved in the same stage of the production process. This type of merger leaves the range of the firm's product unchanged. Horizontal integration enables firms to reap considerable economies of scale. The materials required by the group can be bought in bulk, transport and distribution services can be combined, and the capital reserves of one unit can be used to finance the expansion of another. Amalgamation of firms is also a direct way of reducing competition since it results in a decrease in the number of participants in the market.

There are five major characteristics of marketing groups in agriculture. These are:

(i)   a number of farmers band together to market their produce;
(ii)   the members accept that market requirements will determine what is to be produced;
(iii) the members are willing to accept reasonable restrictions in order to satisfy market requirements;

(iv) the membership of groups is limited to farmers who are large enough, convenient enough, and have sufficient self-discipline to make membership successful;

(v) groups tend to specialize in a small range of commodities.

The objectives of each group normally encompass some or all of the following:

(a) to obtain higher prices, or more realistically, stable prices;

(b) to maintain, or increase their share of the market;

(c) to relieve producers of their individual marketing responsibilities;

(d) to reduce the cost of providing some marketing services and to see that the efficiency of marketing is improved;

(e) to improve the efficiency of production.

Because of the close social cohesion between members, producer groups are better placed to exploit the potential advantages of co-operative assembly, handling, and grading than the traditional impersonal co-operative. The strength of the group lies in the ability to make and keep contracts, with members prepared to accept some measure of control over breeds, varieties, and methods of production.

The initiative for the introduction of groups has come from a variety of sources. The earliest groups were formed to achieve the economies available from bulk buying. The rewards obtained lead to an interest in co-operation in selling as well as in buying. The earliest marketing groups were concerned with livestock production, and have achieved mixed degrees of success. Rather more general success has been achieved by groups involved in the marketing of cereals and potatoes. Here joint ownership of harvesting machinery, storage buildings, and grading plant is feasible.

Encouragement for the formation of groups has come from a number of wholesale and retail companies interested in procuring supplies. The recent rapid development of groups is very much associated with changes in the structure of retailing, particularly the increasing importance of supermarkets for sales of food products. These require regular supplies of graded produce, which can be supplied by properly organized producer groups.

Some marketing co-operatives have groups within their membership. Gloucester Marketing Society (GMS), a horticultural co-operative located in the south west of England, for example, has a number of restricted membership producer groups engaged in the production of horticultural produce to very strict quality standards to meet contracts from a number of large supermarket chains. Members of the groups meet on a regular basis for discussion evenings organized by the co-operative's field officers. As a result of these meetings a close social rapport develops, and members are kept up to date with market requirements.

A large number of groups trade with one member running the group free, however, this is only satisfactory in the short term. As a rule of thumb, within 3 years of its formation a group should be large enough to employ a professional manager. The turnover of the group should enable this, with the management salary not accounting for more than 2½ per cent of the turnover of the group.

The successful producer group is likely to be the one which has precisely-defined objectives. It is also likely to have some precise means of transmitting information from the market to the member, with good overall communications among members. This is likely to take the form of a firm contractual agreement. Professional management, with the duty of influencing production on the farm, is also likely to be a characteristic of a successful group.

Producer groups can be seen, therefore, to have enjoyed greater success in improving the efficiency of the marketing of agricultural produce than have marketing co-operatives. It must be said, though, that an objective measurement of group achievement is very difficult because there are very few norms or standards against which to compare actual results. Overall, marketing groups, although they have their opponents, have undoubtedly had a real impact in the marketing of certain agricultural commodities.

4. *Co-operation in the supply of farmer's requisites*

There is a very long history of farmers joining together to purchase their farm requisites, and a large number of societies have operated, and still do operate, very successfully in this area. The co-operatives differ widely in size, however, the largest requisite society in the United Kingdom, West Cumberland Farmers, has about 30 000 members and a group turnover in excess of £100 million. The range of requisites which can be supplied by the co-operative is virtually unlimited, although certain commodities have come to be of particular significance over recent years. This will be considered in greater detail in Chapter 11.

Groups are again of importance in the supply of requisites. The NFU in England and Wales has been actively concerned with groups from their beginnings and in 1962 helped to form Agricultural Central Trading Co. Ltd. to assist in co-ordinating the groups. The primary purpose of ACT, as it is known, is bulk buying; however, it has also embarked on widespread selling operations through a network of regional trading associations. The early policy of ACT was to buy on the cheapest markets and with the greatest discounts.

The basis of the organization of ACT is that every member is obliged to pay for deliveries promptly. The administration is dealt with centrally at Chesham, and the expense is covered by margins between the manufacturer and the farmer which are kept to a minimum.

Within certain limits, ACT utilizes forward buying, especially of fertilizers. The concept is that farmers should do most of the work themselves in order to reduce costs, that they should plan ahead to buy in bulk, and that they should use ACT as a central agency to buy their bulk orders. ACT holds no stock, and only buys what producers want. The ultimate decision on what happens in each area depends on the farm members. The tendency is to concentrate on what is being done best: buying for farmers, and trying to get the goods from the factory to the farm as efficiently and as economically as possible.

There are at present about 17 000 farmer members, with 700 local groups each electing their own chairman. Each of the chairmen participate in the election of directors on to the Board of each Group Trading Association (GTA), of which there are 14, made up on a county or multi-county basis. They in turn elect their own chairman, and form the Council of ACT. It is the Council's responsibility to elect the Board of ACT.

The 14 GTAs are companies in their own right. Each member subscribes a small loan to ACT on joining and in addition an annual fee is levied. ACT is not a profit-making concern in the accepted sense, however it does have to maintain the Company as a viable unit, making plans for contingencies, and exercising normal commercial prudence.

5. *Federal co-operatives*

The federal co-operative takes the form of an amalgamation of co-operatives which operate together in part, or all, of their business activities. Federal co-operatives have been formed to cover both the marketing of certain commodities and the purchase of selected inputs.

So far as sales are concerned co-operation amongst co-operatives has been most successful in a restricted number of specialist fields. A high proportion of the dessert apples produced in the United Kingdom, for example, are marketed under one brand name. It is a symbol which has become synonymous with a uniform quality of fruit, and is backed up by a highly efficient market intelligence system, with a rigorous control of quality and varieties grown. Its members are both co-operatives marketing top quality fruit on behalf of their members and very large scale individual growers.

Perhaps the most well-known English federal co-operative is Goldenlay, which operates in the egg market. The present membership of Goldenlay comprises West Cumberland Farmers, Yorkshire Egg Producers, and Thames Valley Eggs. Together they account for a considerable share of the total market for eggs and are very active in maintaining the returns of their farming members by employing all aspects of the marketing mix.

On the requisite side, federalization of co-operatives has enabled farmers to develop a share of two product markets where traditionally co-operatives have not played an important part. In 1978 Farmers Crop Chemicals Ltd. was formed, set up by four of the largest co-operatives in the country. This federal operates in the agrochemicals market. In 1979 the largest co-operative in Scotland, North Eastern Farmers, and West Cumberland Farmers, the largest requisite society in England, combined to acquire Hilston Animal Health Services Ltd. This gives a federal co-operative a trading link with the market for pharmaceuticals.

These moves toward federal co-operative trading bodies are industry-wide and should result in an increase in their importance as distribution outlets. There has recently been much discussion over the formation of a 'super co-operative' comprising the biggest national marketing groups, irrespective of product. This concept is seen as an extension of the federalization of co-operatives in an attempt to provide a countervailing power to large multi-national companies operating in the agricultural industry.

The future of agricultural co-operation

As can be seen from the summary of the various types of co-operation which takes place in agriculture, potential exists for co-operatives to play an important part in agricultural management in the United Kingdom. The reasons for this are related to the benefits which are derived from co-operation. The Central Council for Agricultural and Horticultural Co-operation in a policy review (1978) categorized eight major benefits from co-operation which can be summarized as follows:

(i)   reduced costs of inputs or services;
(ii)   improved methods of production;
(iii)   changes in the pattern of production;
(iv)   better facilities for preparing for marketing;
(v)   new market outlets;
(iv)   higher overall returns;
(vii)   greater security, both personal and commercial;
(viii) savings of time and anxiety.

In the light of these benefits it would seem that the future of co-operation is likely to be extremely prosperous. A simple listing of the benefits of co-operation to farmers, however, belies the question of whether co-operatives are actually making any significant improvements in the efficiency of agricultural marketing. Baron (1978) argues that co-operatives have, in fact, achieved only very slight gains in efficiency, and suggests that the major benefits of co-operation lies in the relief of social tensions. Such a relief comes, not in the form of increased profitability for farmer members, but in the short run by providing dominant and innovative farmers with an alternative, and time consuming activity in organizing co-operatives. Such relief works successfully only when tensions are slight, as has happened in the United Kingdom since the 1950s.

It is almost certainly fair to say that co-operation is overrated as a means of improving the efficiency of agricultural marketing. However, because of the huge funds available to encourage its use in British farming, co-operatives will almost certainly increase in size and significance in the future. The major hurdle which must be overcome in order for this to be achieved is the natural independence of the farmer, and his business acumen. The majority of farmers are willing to join co-operatives if they can see commercial advantages in so doing. However, the amount of trading individual members do with their co-operatives varies.

Table 8.2 shows the extent to which a sample of 165 co-operative members in the north of England sold their marketable goods through co-operatives (Foxall and McConnell-Wood 1976).

Table 8.2. The importance of co-operatives
as sources of supply in 1976

Percentage of total requirements obtained from co-operative	Percentage of respondents
76-100	15
51- 75	9
26- 50	8
25 or less	68

Source: Foxall and McConnell-Wood (1976).

The only way in which a greater proportion of trading can be expected to be channelled through co-operatives is as a result of economic justification. In the absence of this, any further major breakthroughs for co-operatives seem unlikely. Groups should have a much more prosperous future, particularly if they have the capital base to provide the grading and processing facilities required by the major purchasers of agricultural commodities.

9. Possibilities for direct marketing by the farmer

Margins in agriculture

Considerable emphasis has been placed in earlier chapters of this book on the fact that, in general, the farmer has an indirect demand for his output, in other words his produce is not bought directly by the final consumer. The way in which the producer and the final consumer are linked is often referred to as the marketing chain. All marketing chains in agriculture can be defined as beginning with production on the farm, and from there on can vary in length considerably, depending on the use to which the commodity is put.

Potatoes, for example, are grown on the farm and are then sold, in some cases directly to the consumer. Alternatively, the potatoes might be sold to a merchant who then sells them to a retailer, who offers them for sale to the final consumer. Another possibility is that the merchant may sell the potatoes to a processor, perhaps for canning, or to make potato crisps, the processed product might then pass through the hands of a wholesaler, before the retailer sells it to the final consumer. These three possible marketing chains for potatoes are illustrated in Fig. 9.1.

(a) Short	(b) Medium	(c) Long
1. Production on farm	1. Production on farm	1. Production on farm
2. Sale direct to consumer	2. Sale to merchant	2. Sale to merchant
	3. Sale to retailer	3. Sale to processor
	4. Sale to consumer	4. Sale to wholesaler
		5. Sale to retailer
		6. Sale to consumer

Fig. 9.1 Possible marketing chains for potatoes.

Similar alternatives exist for the majority of agricultural commodities grown in the United Kingdom. As each commodity progresses along the marketing chain its value increases. The actual extent of the increase in value differs according to particular circumstances, such as the amount of processing required and the degree of competition among firms involved in the industry. The demand for the commodity is also of relevance here. In general, however, the increase in value, whatever its size, is known as the marketing margin.

The marketing margin is therefore the difference between the value of a commodity when it is ready for sale from the farm and its value when it is finally bought by the consumer. The size of the marketing margins which exist in agriculture has been the subject of much investigation and comment. For all agricultural production in the United Kingdom the value added during processing and distribution exceeds the value of food production at the farm level. In 1978, the cost of processing and distributing all food consumed in the United Kingdom, as a percentage of total expenditure on food, amounted to 50.7 per cent. (CSO, 1980). Although this includes imported food, as well as that produced domestically, it gives a good indication of the overall position currently pertaining in agriculture.

The proportion of the final retail value of agricultural commodities which is earned by the farmer varies greatly between agricultural commodities. Shepherd and Futrell (1970), for example, calculated that in 1969, under USA conditions, for grain which was used for bakery and cereal products the farmer's proportion was about 20 per cent. For fruit and vegetables it was around 27 per cent. The farmer received about 50 per cent for milk and dairy products, and between 55 and 60 per cent for meat and eggs.

These proportions give a division between the production and marketing shares of various commodities, with the share enjoyed by an individual farmer depending on his involvement with the marketing of his output. The other point which is worth noting is that the difference in proportions bears little relationship to any differences in the marketing efficiency of the various industries. Grain marketing, for example, is as efficient, if not more so, as egg marketing, the major difference being that grain requires a great deal of processing before it is ready for final consumption, while eggs require relatively little.

Marketing margins, in total, have shown two distinct trends over time. One is that they have persistently increased, the other is that they have shown a degree of consistency to price movements. There are various factors which cause this, principally:

(i)   an increasing volume of food flowing through the system;
(ii) the increasing provision of services with food, particularly a greater degree of processing;
(iii) a proportionately greater increase in marketing costs;
(iv) an increase in the costs of promotion.

It is possible, also, that there are increasing profits accruing to firms which are responsible for marketing agricultural commodities; however, this is not a major causative factor. Beaumont (1971) suggests that because of technological improvements in food marketing, a persistent upward trend in marketing margins is not very evident in the United Kingdom, with added services to the consumer being offset by technological improvements. Beaumont also suggests that increasing margins need not necessarily reflect a decline in farm incomes, because there are a declining number of farmers, and the overall market size is increasing.

In reality, margins fluctuate over time. Meat margins, for example, are both levelled and averaged, which results in more stable prices on the retail market, but occasionally accentuates price fluctuations at the farm level. Levelling is the smoothing of prices from one period to another. The result is that when farm prices are low, retail prices do not decline to the same effect, however, when farm prices are high, butchers take a smaller margin in order to similarly peg their prices. Averaging is the smoothing of margins across different meat products, taking low margins on certain meat cuts in order to stimulate demand, and taking higher margins on other cuts which have a relatively constant demand.

There is a general feeling among farmers that the margins which are added to food products between the farm gate and the final consumer are unsatisfactorily large. In fact there is very little that farmers can do in order to improve their share of the total market for food. Farmers can effectively bargain for improved margins only with the first handlers of their products, however, the greatest part of the costs of marketing is incurred, not at the farmers end of the marketing chain, but at two other points, in the processing plant and at retail level.

The amount which farmers can obtain in the form of increased marketing margins from the first handlers of their products is virtually nil, except in cases where the first handlers add extraordinarily high profits, or add a large amount of value to the product. Moore (1968) worked out the possible improvements in returns to USA farmers making use of countervailing power, through co-operatives and groups, to compete for the first handlers profits for seven agricultural commodities. For three of these commodities there were no improvements to be obtained, and for only wheat for bread was there more than a 1.2 per cent increase available. When the cost of organizing and maintaining an agency for the purpose of bargaining away marketing margins is considered, and also the fact that it almost certainly would not operate as efficiently in practice as in theory, then serious doubts are raised about the validity of farmers' criticisms concerning the excessive margins enjoyed by firms concerned with the marketing of food. The general lack of success of farmers' groups which have attempted to undertake various marketing functions beyond the farm gate gives further evidence of this fact.

Despite the variable successes enjoyed there is still a great deal of support for the notion that farmers should expand their operations beyond the farm gate; this is not only in an attempt to take a share of the elusive margins, but also to give farmers a more assured market, which will hopefully result in improved returns. The basis in theory for such a movement is known as vertical integration, which results from an amalgamation of firms in the marketing chain.

As a result production and marketing decisions are co-ordinated by some firm, or firms, in the industry. These firms are able to specify the kind of product that will be produced, the production practices to be employed, and times and terms of sale. This type of arrangement results in a more uniform product, and provides a high degree of control over the flow of the product through the marketing system.

Vertical integration can take various forms, either backwards towards the raw materials, or forward towards the market. Alternatively, auxiliary goods may be produced by the firm or farm, which were previously produced by outsiders. Vertical integration spreads, or avoids, risks. Advantages accrue from unified control over varying stages of manufacture. More comprehensive planning can be instituted, and there are possible economies of scale resulting from a larger size of business operation. There are also certain possible disadvantages. Problems may result from a basic lack of familiarity with certain techniques, and there may also be a lack of capital for certain operations.

Vertical integration is of direct relevance to agriculture because it plays a major part in the decision making of the vast majority of farmers all around the world. It can be regarded as one of several possible ways in which the small-size structure of agriculture can be adapted to modern marketing techniques. Control can be at any point in the market, however, not all products are suitable for adapting to vertical integration techniques. With poultry, a factory-type enterprise can be adopted with little extra cost and with vastly increased efficiency of production. This is not so feasible, however, for other agricultural commodities.

There are various ways in which vertical integration can be achieved in agriculture, and the most important methods will be considered throughout the remainder of this chapter. It is widely held that farmers who sell through traditional marketing channels are placed in a weak position because of a lack of control over the market. One possibility which exists for reducing the lack of security is for the farmer to enter into a contract with the purchaser of the commodity, or commodities, which he produces. Contracts are used to a varying extent in agriculture, and while they are of considerable importance in certain branches of production, in other areas they are very little used.

Use of contracts

The use of contracts has received great publicity in recent years, although it is not an entirely recent phenomenon and has been in common use since the end of the First World War. At that time, however, most market deals were sealed by the shake of a hand, or the fall of the auctioneer's hammer. In the mid-1930s corn merchants began to issue written sale notes confirming verbal agreements made in the weekly corn exchange. From this beginning developed the formalized practice of forward contracting. A similar development has occurred for other agricultural commodities.

In 1971 the importance of the use of contracts as a means of stabilizing the marketing of agricultural products was recognized by the appointment, in the UK, of a Committee of Inquiry on Contract Farming under the chairmanship of Sir James Barker

(Barker Report 1972). The Committee viewed a contract, in its widest sense, as being

> a commitment to provide an agricultural commodity of a type, at a time, and in the quantity required by a known buyer. Such production often involves some degree of transferred management responsibility, and with it some degree of transfer of the commercial risk. It is also necessary that there should be some stated basis for fixing the price at which the produce is to change hands.

The Committee concluded that contracting has had, on the whole, a favourable influence on farming in the past, and that this is likely to continue in the future. Thus there is scope for an expansion in the use of contracts in agriculture, together with an increase in the degree of horizontal groupings of farmers. The Committee recognized that since consumer demand can never be totally predicted, there will always be some room for speculative production. However, in the main contract production is a suitable mechanism for procuring the bulk of agricultural commodities which are produced.

Three major types of contract are used in British agriculture. These can be classified as:

1. Marketing contracts, covering the sale of a product which has either been produced, or is in the process of being produced. The terms usually concern the price, quality and quantity of the product and the time of delivery. The buyer has no control over production techniques. Contracts of this type are fairly common for arable products.
2. Buying contracts, covering the purchase of farm inputs for use in agricultural or horticultural production. Typical contracts in this area cover the purchase of feeding stuffs by farmers.
3. Transferred management contracts, transferring part, or all, of the farmer's management responsibilities to the buyer. The degree of transfer varies, for seed-corn production, for example, the control may only extend to type of seed and crop sprays used, and the timing of applications, while for broiler chicken production the buyer may own the buldings used, supply the animals and feeding-stuffs and dictate production targets and delivery dates.

Whatever the type of contract used, the most crucial aspect will always be the price of the commodity. Various methods of price fixing are common-place in contracts, with four of major importance. The simplest method is to have a fixed price written into the contract which will be adhered to by both parties regardless of fluctuations in trading levels after the contract has been signed and before it is completed. The use of a fixed price transfers the risks of trading from the farmer to the buyer since the farmer knows in advance exactly what he will receive for his output. Alternatively, prices can be based on some agreed addition to the farmer's production costs. This gives very good security, particularly if it is coupled with a rise or fall clause, relating to market prices.

Another method used is for prices to be fixed at some agreed addition to, or reduction from, prevailing market prices. This increases the farmer's risk, as does the final alternative which is for the price to be determined at the time of sale. Here the only security offered to the farmer is that he will have a market for his produce, which is essential for certain agricultural commodities such as sugar beet and oil seed rape.

Overall, contracts are becoming increasingly in the interests of farmers. However, there are disadvantages, as well as advantages, associated with their use. The advantages can be summarized as follows:

(i)   The farmer has a reasonably assured market for his produce at a reasonably assured price.

(ii) The assured prices allow the use of a more sophisticated planning procedure in farm management planning.

(iii) When quality is specified there will almost certainly be a premium offered.

(iv) Premia for other services will also be available, for example, regular supply of a commodity.

(v)   The farmer will be kept informed of any possible improvements in production techniques.

(vi) For some commodities, contracts will be virtually the only way to sell the product. An example is in the production of vining peas. Because of the costs involved in production and harvesting very few farmers grow the crop unless they have a contract with a processing firm before planting takes place.

The disadvantages of contracts are closely related to the advantages:

(i)   The farmer will be less able to take the opportunity of windfall profits which might arise in the case of some short-term market oddity such as happened in the UK potato market in 1975 and 1976.

(ii) The buyer may insist on particular methods of production, and certain selected inputs being used. These might possibly increase the costs of production, without compensatory improvements in returns.

(iii) The buyer is carrying most of the risk, thus he will tend to offset this by encouraging the farmer to make continual improvements in techniques and efficiency.

(iv) There may be penalties for poor quality, outweighing any premia for high quality.

(v)   Contracts are rarely signed for more than a year and if the buyer fails to take up his contract there is little that the farmer can do. Contracts do not give anyone complete security, thus an enormous investment in fixed capital may not be justified.

One of the areas of greatest potential with regard to the use of contracts by farmers lies in the disposal of arable crops. There are two major methods by which arable products are traded; through spot sales and via the use of forward contracts. Most farmers store their grain after harvest and then sell over the winter months, either as tradition dictates, or when marketing conditions indicate that a sale should be made. Spot sales occur when a farmer and a merchant agree on a deal for the immediate sale of a consignment of grain. The agreement will normally be verbal, based on mutual trust. An alternative possibility is for them to agree on a sale which will be completed at some time in the future, for example a deal might be agreed while the grain is still growing in the field, to be completed at some time after harvesting has taken place.

The various aspects of the deal will be laid down in a formal contract. These include:

(i)   method by which the price is to be agreed;
(ii) time of delivery of the grain;
(iii) tonnage of grain covered by the agreement;
(iv) minimum acceptable quality of the grain;
(v)   time and method of payment for the grain.

Normally a fixed price will be written into the forward contract, and this price will be paid regardless of the level of 'spot' prices at the time the contract is completed. This is made possible by the use of futures contracts by agricultural merchants.

A futures contract, like a forward contract, is a legally binding agreement by which one party undertakes to deliver grain at a specified date in the future, and the other party agrees to take delivery at that date. However, the futures contract, unlike the forward contract, is negotiable, and can be sold at the currently ruling price for such transactions. Futures trading does not, therefore, necessarily involve the physical transfer of a commodity. A trader who has made a contract to sell can offset it by purchasing a contract to buy the same amount of grain.

Agricultural merchants who operate in this way when taking out forward contracts act as 'hedgers', balancing price changes on spot or forward dealings by a simultaneous dealing in futures. The large-scale agricultural merchanting firms, in particular the national feed compounders, may simultaneously operate as 'speculators' in the futures market, deliberately leaving themselves open to price changes and attempting to take advantage of them by skilful buying and selling of contracts. These two methods of dealing will, however, take place quite separately.

In the UK there are two separate and independent cereals futures markets, at London and at Liverpool. The London Baltic Exchange allows trading in contracts for home-grown barley and wheat, and contracts made at Liverpool relate to home-grown barley. Futures contracts are, therefore, available only for wheat and barley of *feeding* quality, and are not available for other grains, such as barley of malting specification. For these grains forward contract prices are set as a result of the prices negotiated weekly between merchants and end users for bulk lots. Local corn markets are not used to a sufficient extent to play an important part in price determination.

Traditionally there has been a great deal of mistrust of farmers with regard to the use of forward contracts. This has come about mainly as a result of price fluctuations between the date of the contract being signed and the date of delivery. In a national survey of farmers undertaken by the author in 1978, farmers were asked whether they had ever used forward contracts for grain, and if they had, whether they still used them. Of the farmers interviewed, 43 per cent of those who produced arable crops had at some time or another used forward contracts for grain sales. Of that proportion,

69 per cent still used forward contracts, and were happy with them, the remainder had ceased to use them for a variety of reasons, chiefly as a result of being let down by merchants when the market price turned out to be below the forward price agreed in the contract. This suggests that there is potential for more responsible merchant behaviour in grain trading.

There have also been criticisms levelled against futures markets, chiefly as a result of the conflicting operations of hedgers and speculators. The speculator deliberately exposes himself to risk, buying and selling futures contracts and rarely, if ever, handling physical quantities of the commodity described in the contract. The aim of the dealing is to make a profit out of price changes in the futures market.

Various futures markets exist for commodities in the UK, ranging from cocoa and coffee to copper and tin. Specific rules of conduct are required of the market in order to maintain fair trading standards. Necessary prerequisites for successful trading include:

(i)   excellent communications;
(ii) efficient standardization and classification procedures for the products traded;
(iii) adequate market information;
(iv) the exchange must provide a means of evaluating credit standing, certifying standards, and settling disputes.

It is possible for the operation of speculators to accentuate price fluctuations, particularly if a 'squeeze' occurs with a market participant buying up a large quantity of the futures contracts relating to a particular month and thus controlling a large proportion of the supply of the commodity. At the end of the month speculators who hold contracts for which they do not have physical stocks of the commodity have to buy from the squeezer, usually at very high prices. Elaborate rules have been introduced in an endeavour to avoid this type of market operation.

In 1957, there was much controversy in the USA with regard to the effects of futures trading on commodity prices, when a wave of speculation in onion futures resulted in a virtual doubling of the price of onions within the space of a few days. As a result of protests, a hearing was held, and subsequently futures trading in onions was banned by law. After the market was closed Working (1960) undertook an intensive study of the data relating to the onions futures market and found a clear indication that, overall, futures trading in onions had substantially reduced the amount of variation in spot prices. Shepherd and Futrell (1970) have shown that as the volume of futures trading increases so does the number of spot price changes, however, this is different from the volume of price changes. In contrast, a Home-Grown Cereals Authority (1978) study of London futures trading in barley found that the lightest trading day of the week, Monday, was also the day with the largest daily recorded price fluctuations.

In general small-scale speculators lose and large scale speculators make money. In the UK, the classic example of the potential cost of speculation relates to the experience of Rowntrees Ltd., operating in the cocoas futures market, and widely reported thereafter in the popular press. Their traders sold a large number of futures contracts on the hunch that prices were likely to go down, in which case they would buy them off the market before they had to supply any cocoa to fulfil the contract, at a profit to themselves. In fact the price of cocoa went up significantly, and the contracts had to be bought back off the market at seven times the price for which they were sold. The cost, to Rowntrees, of the exercise has been estimated to be about £28 million.

In the UK it is suggested that comparatively little use is made of futures markets in agriculture. The reasons for this are varied. Traditionally Government stabilization schemes and the existence of statutory marketing boards have reduced the need for futures markets. There is also a problem of definition of products, because of very great quality variations within particular commodities. In addition, the standard of market information provided relating to agricultural commodities is, on the whole, very poor.

For feeding wheat and feeding barley the level of forward trading varies according to the likely size of the new crop harvest. In years when growers feel that the following crop will be good, and therefore market prices low, they are often inclined to take out a forward contract for part or all of their output, as an insurance policy against the probably low prices. In 1978, for example, UK harvest predictions were very high, and trading levels for forward contracts were also particularly buoyant. In years of poor harvests, conversely, spot market prices are inclined to increase substantially once the actual extent of the harvest level is ascertained, reducing the need for, and the attractiveness to the farmer of, a forward contract. In 1976, the UK harvest was disappointing, and farmers holding forward contracts lost out by up to £10 per tonne in comparison to spot prices.

The use of contracts, then, is an important part of the marketing activity of the farmer, enabling him to reduce his trading risks and increase the security of his financial returns. Whilst not completely shielding him, they do offer a significant benefit, in terms of reducing his dependence on the uncertain vagaries of agricultural markets. It must always be remembered, however, that a contract is only a piece of paper and as such is open to misinterpretation and manipulation, possibly to the detriment of both parties to the agreement.

Sales direct to the consumer

The other major possibility which exists for the individual farmer who wishes to undertake some form of vertical integration is for him to consider sales direct to the consumer. It is often said that patterns of farming go in cycles. Whether or not this is true, one of the greatest areas of development in farming at the present time is the upsurge of interest in direct farm sales. Direct selling is not an innovation, having been established in areas such as the Vale of Evesham and East Anglia for many years. However, it has only recently become popular on a national basis in the UK.

There are various reasons for this upsurge in interest. Possibly the most important is the consistent desire of farmers to achieve higher returns from the market, which has become a feasible proposition because of the vast increase in the sales of deep freezers. This has created a demand for large quantities of soft fruits and vegetables. At the same time there has been an increase in the popularity of leisure motoring by town dwellers venturing into the countryside. From the consumer point of view, properly organized direct farm sales undoubtedly satisfy their requirements for fresh, good quality farm produce, giving value for money, and purchased in rural surroundings.

Marketing direct to the consumer can take different forms; however, whichever type of direct selling is envisaged there are various general factors which should be borne in mind. Some of the most important of these are:

1. Location—direct selling is more likely to be successful if there

are urban centres of population within reasonable driving distance of the farm, and if the farm is near to, or on a well-used and maintained road. Access to the farm from the road is very important, and may require planning permission; serious consideration must also be given to competition from similar businesses which are already established in the area. This is likely to become increasingly important as the popularity of direct marketing by farmers increases over the years. Research by the author has shown that there is already evidence of keen price competition between self-pick strawberry proprietors in certain parts of the country (Barker 1980).

2. Effect on the farm, family and staff—undertaking direct selling changes the nature of the farm from a production unit to a production and selling enterprise. This may entail working long and unsocial hours, especially at weekends. Also farm families are not usually trained in retail selling, and a greater degree of tolerance than farmers normally exercise is an essential prerequisite of a successful endeavour. In certain cases the farm staff may not be amenable to working on a new venture such as direct marketing. Some farmers prefer to hire casual labour, particularly students, and leave the farm staff to carry on with the routine work.

3. Effect on the farm business—serious consideration must be given to the effect which direct selling will have on the rest of the farm business. There can at times be serious conflicts between normal farming operations and the direct selling enterprise. Labour requirements, in particular, may cause stress at busy times. Also, cropping for successional harvesting may impinge on what has been previously a settled rotational system, and cause problems which have not been experienced before.

There are four principle methods of marketing direct to the consumer, all of which will be considered in detail in the remainder of this chapter. The methods are back-door sales, sales through a farm-based shop or stall, self-pick or pick-your-own enterprises, and farmer-run shops or garden centres located at sites other than on the farm premises.

1. *Back-door sales*

Back-door sales need not be covered in any great detail. They are usually an incidental activity to the farm business, of an informal nature, providing unofficial extra income for the farmer's wife.

The only major problem with this type of sale is that customers can arrive at any time, which can occasionally be inconvenient.

There is little risk involved with this type of selling because any surplus not sold can be sent through the normal wholesale channels. Commodities which can be sold by this means include eggs, poultry, fruit, vegetables, and potatoes.

There is frequently an advantage of up to 25 per cent over normal wholesale prices, which can more than double the profit potential from the enterprise, not taking into account the cost of family labour.

2. *Farm shops or stalls*

A much greater degree of commitment is required if it is decided to introduce a farm shop or stall to the farm business. Farm shops vary in their degree of sophistication, and may be associated with other enterprises such as self-pick operations, camping sites, recreation areas and so on. The aim is usually to obtain a regular throughput and income throughout the year. However, the shops may be kept open all the year round, or open seasonally, depending on individual circumstances.

Retailing produce is covered by law. There are various Acts of relevance, and anyone setting up a farm shop is well advised to consult the relevant department of the Local Authority before embarking on a project. A recent survey by the author of farmers undertaking direct marketing indicates that the range of goods stocked by farm shops is considerable, covering fresh and frozen meat and poultry, flowers, potatoes, fresh and frozen vegetables, eggs, milk, butter and dairy produce, cooked foods, and other non-food products, particularly samples of local crafts. Planning consent is not required to start a farm shop provided that the goods offered for sale are grown on the holding, and the shop premises are part of the existing farm buildings.

With regard to the presentation of the products, the general atmosphere should be bright and clean. A high standard of personal hygiene for the operator and assistants is essential.

Greater care needs to be exercised when selling meat and poultry products; however, substantial rewards are available as an incentive. It may be useful to secure the services of an experienced butcher, or to undertake an agreement with a local abbatoir. The sale of meat for the home freezer involves the use of a schedule showing what is available. If a delivery service is being considered this needs careful consideration to ensure that costs can be met. It must be borne in mind that opportunities in meat retailing are few, and competition is likely to be fierce.

The capital cost of setting up a farm shop can be high if the public authorities require the buildings to be brought up to the standards required under the Shops and Offices Act. The shop will require constant supervision, entailing at least one full-time employee, and other operating costs including heating, lighting, display counters, scales, and cash registers. If the range of products sold becomes large then it is important to keep an account of all products sold, checking the percentage of trade, and the amount of profit contributed to the business.

For a farm stall to operate successfully it should, as mentioned earlier, be sited adjacent to roads with a high traffic flow, or near to urban areas. Holiday routes are favourite locations, and selling from stalls is usually of a seasonal nature. The range of farm stalls tends to be restricted exclusively to fruit, fresh vegetables, flowers, and potatoes. Farm stalls can be any sort of temporary structure, ranging from a trestle table to a farm trailer. So long as it is a moveable structure it may, in the UK, be erected without planning permission for 28 consecutive days, or 14 two-day weekends, or any other combination of 28 days, but to satisfy the law as to its temporary nature it should not be allowed to remain for periods exceeding a total of 4 weeks whether used or not.

Farm stalls suffer very damaging competition from opportunists who set up sales points in lay-bys of busy roads and sell substandard fruit and vegetables from them. This has damaged the reputation of farm-sold products and emphasizes the fact that the stall should not be regarded as a place to dispose of lower quality produce; rather it should be attractively dressed and scrupulously clean. The major resource required in such an enterprise is labour. The stall needs to be continuously manned, and a pleasant salesperson can have a definite positive effect in encouraging repeat visits.

3. *Self-pick or pick-your-own crops*

Self-pick or pick-your-own is a further direct marketing option. In this area there is virtually no reasonable limit to the range of crops which can be grown successfully, from well-proven soft fruit and potatoes through to exotic vegetables such as courgettes. The old marketing maxim, 'if the customer wants it, we stock it' can usefully be applied here. It is essential that the crops are grown to a high standard. The public particularly dislike poor quality produce, these just do not get picked; also weeds, which can make picking wet and difficult; and the presence of pests and diseased fruit.

Some sort of provision for parking cars must be made, this usually being a reasonably adjacent, recently cut, grass field—preferably without too many cow pats! For larger enterprises, marshals are normally provided to ensure the orderly parking of cars. It is also a good idea to provide toilet facilities, especially for ladies. Portable lavatories can be hired. In certain cases in the U.S.A. (Teichman 1975) it has been discovered that an old fashioned outside privy becomes an attraction to customers in its own right! If the self-pick enterprise is a reasonable size it is probably in the proprietor's interests to provide a children's play area. This will reduce the possibility that while parents are picking fruit, their children will be creating havoc around the farm.

In the field, the fruit and vegetables should be grown in well-spaced rows to enable easy picking, and it is important to plan well ahead so that adjacent plots ripen together, rather than having pickers all over the farm. It is essential to place check-out points very carefully. This speeds up customer flow and minimizes dishonesty.

Capital requirements for self-pick enterprises are reasonable, apart from the costs of introducing the crops to the farm rotation. Basic requirements are a good set of scales, which meet Local Authority regulations, a large table or bench for the check-out, and containers for picking into. It is desirable to provide picking containers of a standard size and weight. These should be durable and hygienic, which almost certainly means plastic, unless give-away cardboard baskets are provided.

An inevitable problem is the amount of fruit that customers eat while they are picking. The proprietors of a self-pick site in Ireland (Bowbrick and Twohig 1977) found that children in particular frequently make no pretence at filling a punnet. The more people that come in a party the more is eaten for every sale. The most flagrant case discovered was a family who brought along six children and plentiful supplies of sugar and cream.

4. *Farmer-run shops and garden centres*

The final possibility for direct marketing to be covered in this section involves moving beyond the bounds of the farm gate by setting up shops or garden centres as totally separate enterprises in centres of population. To set up a garden centre involves moving into a business environment which will be very unlike that of farming, while farmer-run shops are an extension of the 'if the mountain won't come to Mohamet, then Mohamet must go to the mountain' principle. As examples of this, in England, a North Yorkshire pig producer has opened a butcher's shop in a nearby Cleveland town, channelling part of his production through it, and a group of Berkshire farmers have taken over a corner shop on a busy local road to provide an outlet for their meat, vegetables, and dairy produce.

Most farmer-run shops and garden centres do not exclusively sell produce which has been grown on the home farms. It is important to provide a balanced supply, buying-in stock when home produce is out of season. It is possible in certain circumstances to build up a consumer preference for home-grown produce and this can be translated gradually into a price premium.

It has been estimated that more than three quarters of households in Britain have a garden. Their needs are supplied by nurserymen, chain stores, hardware stores, and garden centres. There is considerable competition between these sectors, and several garden centres have gone bankrupt as a result. Any farmer or nurseryman considering setting up a garden centre requires sound business sense, a great deal of capital and the ability to cope with a great deal of paperwork. Orientation towards marketing is more important than an ability to grow plants.

The site should be within easy reach of a fairly large population and planning consent is necessary. Car parking must be provided, and mains water, electricity, and toilets are essentials. Again it may be prudent to provide a children's playground.

Seeds and sundries can normally be purchased on a sale or return basis which reduces some of the risks from trading. Other profitable lines include garden chemicals, and agencies for such products as garden sheds, greenhouses, lawnmowers, garden tools and so on. Setting up a garden centre is no light undertaking, and requires high capital investment. At the same time, however, it offers good rewards to the successful entrepreneur, with mark ups, (that is the difference between the price which is paid for a commodity, and the price at which it is sold to the consumer) varying between 50 and 100 per cent.

General considerations regarding direct marketing

There are various general considerations which should be borne in mind by any farmer contemplating undertaking direct marketing. One of the most important aspects is the legal requirements governing direct sales. Some of the most important Acts of relevance in the UK include the following:

1. *The Weights and Measures Act 1963*
   (i)   Any weighing or measuring equipment must be passed as fit for use by an Inspector of the local Weights and Measures Department of the County Council.
   (ii) Selling by weight or quantity is also governed by the Act, there being different conditions for different produce.
2. *The Health and Safety at Work Act 1974*
   (i)   Any sales premises must be safe and without risk to health. The maintenance of this requirement is the responsibility of the proprietor.
3. *Food Hygiene (General) Regulations 1970* and
   Market, Stalls, and Delivery Amendment Regulations 1966
   (i)   These control the sales of soft drinks, ice creams, and other refreshments.
4. *The Occupiers Liability Act 1957*
   (i)   This makes the occupier liable for any accident or injury suffered by a third party who has been invited on to his land. It is important to ensure that adequate insurance is taken out to cover this liability.
5. *Shops Act 1950*
   All Sunday trading is forbidden, apart from a number of exceptions, including:
   (i)   flowers, fresh fruit, and fresh vegetables;
   (ii) milk and cream;
   (iii) newly cooked provisions.

In addition, VAT regulations must be observed if turnover exceeds £5000 per annum. If cider or perry is manufactured and sold, registration with Her Majesty's Customs and Excise Department must be made and duty is payable.

The situation with regard to planning and rating requirements is rather confused. The extent of control depends on the nature of the outlet, and before any venture is put into operation it would be pertinent to seek the advice of a local ADAS, NFU or other official to check on the likely position with regard to planning and rates. A general rule of thumb is that the only occasions where planning permission is not required, and rating is not applicable, is if existing buildings only are used for the enterprise, and only home produced commodities are sold.

Advertising and sales promotion are of crucial importance in direct marketing. It is no good providing facilities which no one knows about, however, similarly it is important to be able to cater for any demand produced as a result of promotions. Table 9.1 shows the types of advertising used by farmers undertaking direct marketing interviewed by the author in 1978.

Table 9.1. Types of advertising used by farmers undertaking direct marketing in 1978

Advertising used	All farmers	Farm shops	Self-pick
Local daily newspaper	42	22	33
Local weekly newspaper	43	24	35
Posters	6	1	6
Direct mail	2	1	1
Local radio	3	1	3
Road signs	100	68	55
None at all	6	4	1
	($n = 118$)	($n = 73$)	($n = 61$)

Source: unpublished research by the author.

One hundred and eighteen farmers from two regions, the North East and the West Midlands regions of England, were visited and asked, among other things, the type of advertising which they used to publicize their direct selling enterprise. Advertising was predominantly in local daily and weekly newspapers and by the use of road signs. There is probably as great a danger of over-advertising as under-advertising. There have been several instances (Fabian 1972; Moore 1970; Cobbledick 1974) of customers causing traffic jams and the occasioning considerable damage to farm property when they arrive to find a self-pick area without any ripe fruit.

In addition to advertising there is a wide variety of sales promotion techniques available to farmers who are marketing direct to the customer. Some of the more common are give-away key rings and car stickers, polythene bags and punnets bearing the name of the farm shop or pick-your-own enterprise and for farm shops, special offers and national-brand grocery promotions.

Considerable importance is placed by many farmers on the image or impression which direct selling gives to customers. Of the farmers interviewed in the author's survey, 86 per cent of respondents felt that their image was important. Two particular aspects were stressed, fresh, top quality produce, and good value, good service, and a friendly attitude to customers.

Farmers taking part in the survey were also asked towards whom in particular their advertising was aimed. The most frequently mentioned sectors were tourists, housewives, and town dwellers.

Pricing is another consideration which is of great importance in direct sales enterprises. It is a crucial factor, and the greatest problem, common to all methods of direct marketing, is how to set prices of the goods to be sold. Some people suggest that prices should be held constant throughout the season. The farmers interviewed in the survey were asked how they decided on the price to charge for their goods. Table 9.2 gives an indication of pricing policy.

Table 9.2. Methods of pricing used by farmers undertaking direct marketing in 1978

Pricing policy	Number of respondents
Refer to local wholesale prices	26
Keep in line with shop prices	19
Set the price for each product in relation to its current supply and demand	5
Add a margin to the cost of production	6
Some combination of the above	43
	($n = 116$)

Source: unpublished research by the author.

Table 9.2 shows the variety of methods used by farmers to decide on the prices to charge for their products. Perhaps the most popular method is to set the price somewhere between local wholesale and retail prices.

The problems associated with undertaking direct marketing are varied. As in all farming the weather plays a very important part in determining the success or otherwise of the enterprise. Farmers who are tenants should make sure with their landlord that they will not break their tenancy agreements by undertaking direct marketing. It is also essential to keep an accurate cash sales ledger, as there is always the possibility that one of the customers may be the local tax inspector.

The final aspect to be considered is perhaps the most important: the future prospects for direct selling. As in all parts of farming the future popularity of direct marketing is very much related to its present profitability and the profits which are likely to be available in the future.

There is very little available information concerning actual profits which have been made by farmers undertaking direct marketing enterprises. Reading University undertook a survey of the farm shop which they run and found that the increased margin over normal available market returns varied from 19 per cent for eggs to 32 per cent for flowers, fruit, and vegetables. However, because eggs accounted for by far the greatest proportion of trade, they did, in fact, give a 66 per cent contribution to the total gross profits of the shop, as opposed to the 15 per cent contribution from flowers, fruit, and vegetables.

For self-pick enterprises there is very little available information concerning actual returns. However, in 1979 for strawberry and raspberry crops, given very variable conditions between different enterprises, a return of £676 per acre of strawberries was feasible at a price of 30p per lb and for raspberries a return of £616 per acre at a price of 35p per lb. It must be noted that for strawberries, in the case of a price war, if prices were reduced to 16p per lb, the associated returns would be minus £30 per acre based on a similar calculation [for detailed calculations and conditions see Barker (1980)].

In the United Kingdom at the present time, many farmers are entering direct marketing. Nobody, as yet, knows how many participants the market can bear. Experience shows that competition can be both healthy, and disastrous if it is taken too far. Because of this the future of direct marketing is uncertain.

Under certain circumstances, missing out the traditional links in the marketing chain offers the farmer a real opportunity to get an improved return from the market. However, marketing direct to the consumer may produce more problems than it solves, although that is not to say that farmers cannot and should not undertake such a venture. In general, any increase in marketing responsibility is viewed by the farmer with mistrust. Direct selling requires a large scale increase in marketing responsibility, and although farmshops, self-pick crops and farmer-run shops or garden centres may all seem attractive propositions, any inclusion of direct sales into the farm business should be planned with great deliberation. Basically the farmer should 'look before he leaps' in order to avoid a financially perilous fall.

Summary

It can be seen from the methods of marketing reviewed in this chapter that there are various openings available to farmers to sell their products in ways other than through the traditional channels. It is often suggested that the only way by which farmers can effectively organize the marketing of their produce is through the use of co-operatives. This is patently not true. Co-operatives are, in certain cases, playing a very effective part in improving the marketing expertise, and the returns from marketing, of farmers. However, such benefits can be enjoyed equally by farmers operating independently. Much depends on the nature of the product, and the extent and quality of the individual farmer's resources. Perhaps the most important fact which can be gained from this review is that direct sales demonstrate the possibilities which exist for individual farmers to apply marketing principles in the management of their businesses.

Part IV. The application of marketing principles to the purchase of agricultural inputs

10. The market for agricultural inputs

The size of the market for farm inputs has increased dramatically in recent years, mainly as a result of inflation, improvements in technology, and increased mechanization. By 1978 the value of the market extended to over £3900 million (CSO 1980). The potential for planned marketing in the acquisition of farm requisites is extensive, and in this chapter the various methods of distribution used to supply the farmer will be examined in an endeavour to identify possibilities for farmers to organize and improve the efficiency of the marketing of their inputs. Initially, however, the structure of British agriculture will be considered briefly, particularly the characteristics of farmers, in order to produce a better understanding of the nature of both the market for agricultural inputs and the farmer as a customer.

Changes in the structure of UK agriculture over time

In recent years there have been various changes occurring in the structure of British agriculture which are likely to affect the market for farm inputs. Some of the most important of these changes include the following:

1. A reduction in the number of farms, and an increase in the average size of those remaining. In 1969 there were 315 000 registered holdings in the United Kingdom, and by 1977 this had diminished to 261 000 (MAFF 1978). Part of this reduction is as a result of loss of land to industry, and residential development, however, the rest is explained by an amalgamation of holdings, resulting in a continuously increasing average size of farm. In 1975 the average size was 111 hectares and by 1977 this had increased to 113 hectares. The impact of this is that there will be fewer farmer customers for agricultural inputs, however those remaining will be of a larger scale.

2. There is a tendency towards greater specialization, with a definite trend towards increasing size, and scale, of enterprises. This is very well illustrated by the situation in dairying. Table 10.1 shows the increasing importance of large dairy herds over the last 10 years.

Table 10.1. Increasing importance of dairy herds of over 50 cows in the UK from 1969 to 1977

	1969	1974	1977
Percentage of herds having more than 50 cows	18.3	31.6	35.6
Percentage of total cows contained in herds of over 50 cows	44.3	62.4	66.4

Source: MMB (1979).

Large-scale units are therefore of very great importance to the suppliers of farm requisites, since they are responsible for an increasing proportion of the total market.

3. There is a continuous reduction in the size of the agricultural labour force, and an accompanying increase in the level of mechanization. The situation has changed considerably from the early nineteenth century when one third of the total labour force was employed in agriculture, to the present time when less than 3 per cent of the total UK work force finds its employment in farming. There are many reasons for this dramatic change of emphasis. Its importance in the context of the changing structure of the market for farm inputs, however, is that there is an ever increasing demand for machinery which can be used to replace manpower on the farm.

4. There are continuous changes in the popularity and importance of different enterprises on farms. In recent years the acreages of oats and potatoes have declined, being replaced by crops such as fodder maize, oilseed rape, and particularly winter barley in the late 1970s. This has considerable impact on the market for agricultural requisites, in terms of both different husbandry requirements, and different types of machinery.

5. There is an associated intensification of, particularly, cropping and grass production. This has particular significance for manufacturers of requisites such as fertilizers, herbicides, and pesticides, with demand continually increasing.

6. There are some moves towards greater self sufficiency, reflected in reduced sales of cereals from farms, an increased use of on-farm milling and mixing, and reduced sales of compound feeds.

Such changes in the pattern of agriculture are unlikely to change the total market very much, however, individual products may be greatly affected by changes such as the banning of the insecticide DDT, and the reduction in the importance of the heavy horse. The current situation in British agriculture, as a result of the changes previously discussed, is that in 1977 the amount of money spent by UK farmers on agricultural inputs was estimated to be as shown in Table 10.2.

Table 10.2. Expenditure, by UK farmers, on major agricultural inputs in 1977

Requisite commodity	Expenditure (£m)
Feeding-stuffs	1785
Fertilizers	422
Fuel and oils	191
Machinery	476
Seeds	208

Source: CSO (1980).

This immediately shows up the overriding importance of the feeding-stuffs industry, and because of this compound feeds hold a dominant position in the agricultural distributive trade.

Characteristics of UK farmers

A lot of prominence is given to the nature of the farmer as a customer. In general, he is held to be rather different from industrial purchasers, and this is partly the result of the characteristics of the participants in the industry, particularly the age structure, level of education, number of years in farming, number of years of managerial experience, and relative geographical immobility. The figures which will be referred to in the following discussion of the characteristics of UK farmers are all based on a random sample of 475 UK farmers interviewed by the author in 1978 and 1979.

Table 10.3. shows the age structure of the farmers interviewed.

Table 10.3. Age structure of UK farmers in 1978-9

Age group	Percentage of respondents
less than 35	20
35-44	21
45-54	29
55-64	20
65 and over	10

Source: Unpublished research by the author.

On the basis of this sample, therefore, it can be seen that almost 60 per cent of farmers in the United Kingdom are aged 45 or over, and over one tenth of the farms are managed by people over the official age of retirement. This is reflected in Table 10.4 which shows the number of years in farming of the farmers interviewed.

Table 10.4. Number of years of farming experience of UK farmers in 1978/79

Number of years	Percentage of respondents
Less than 10	13
11-20	21
21-30	27
31-40	18
41-50	12
More than 50	9

Source: Unpublished research by the author.

There is, as a result, a wealth of experience among farmers, accrued as a result of years of participation in the industry. The general tradition is that most farmers serve a very long apprenticeship before taking over the management of the farm, usually under the guidance of some older member of his family. The result is that the average number of years of management experience, as shown in Table 10.5, is considerably less than the number of years in farming.

Table 10.5. Number of years of management experience
of UK farmers in 1978/79

Number of years	Percentage of respondents
Less than 10	22
11-20	25
21-30	30
31-40	18
41-50	4
More than 50	1

Source: Unpublished research by the author.

An interesting insight into the nature of the farmer as a customer
is given by a consideration of the level of education common
among farmers. Table 10.6 shows the last place of education
attended by the farmers interviewed.

Table 10.6. Last place of education attended
by UK farmers in 1978/79

Last place of education attended	Percentage of respondents
Village school	21
Secondary education	52
Technical or Commercial College	6
Agricultural College	11
University or Polytechnic	8
Other	2

Source: Unpublished research by the author.

Over 70 per cent of the farmers interviewed had had no formal
education beyond that legally required of them. There is also evidence of a lack of geographical mobility among farmers. A Gallup
Poll in 1964 found that 25 per cent of farmers had spent 21-30 years
on the same farm, and a further 25 per cent had spent 31 or more
years on the same holdings.

All of these characteristics are likely to affect the attitudes of
farmers towards the purchase of their inputs. The typical UK
farmer can be viewed as relatively old, with a wealth of farming
experience, and considerable managerial experience. He is also

likely to have a relatively low level of formal education, and to be geographically immobile. In general, farmers are regarded as being conservative in outlook, and resistant to changes in technology and suppliers.

At the same time, however, the majority of farmers are quite willing to consider viable alternatives, and to listen to the advice of anybody whom they consider to be knowledgeable and responsible. Farmers also tend to be very loyal to their suppliers. Two thirds of the farmers interviewed claimed always to buy their fertilizers from the same supplier, and this loyalty is likely to continue so long as their trust is returned.

The foregoing, therefore, gives a very brief outline of the farmer as a purchaser, rather than as a seller. In the light of this, consideration will now be given to the most important methods of distribution used in the supply of farm inputs.

Methods of distribution used to supply the farmer

There are various distribution channels in the United Kingdom which are available to the manufacturers of farm requisites. Six distinctive methods can be identified, namely:

1. Direct selling,
2. sales through agricultural merchants,
3. commission agents,
4. farmer buying groups,
5. direct mail,
6. miscellaneous methods.

Initially a review of these distribution methods will be undertaken, looking at their advantages and disadvantages from the point of view of the manufacturer. This will be followed by a discussion of their present, and likely future, utilization in the most important sectors of the market for farmer's requisites.

1. *Direct selling*

The manufacturer who undertakes direct selling is responsible for every aspect of marketing and distribution. The major advantages of this are:

1. There is a high degree of control over the marketing of the product.

2. Salesmen devote all their time to selling the product or products of the manufacturer. This avoids less than complimentary comparisons being made with regard to the quality of competitors' products.
3. There is direct control of the salesmen employed, they can be trained with regard to company policy, and will therefore have a certain standard of product knowledge.
4. There will be direct contact with the customer, giving a good return of market intelligence, for example, with regard to customers' reactions, and competitors' movements and policies.

There are also, however, associated disadvantages, some of the main ones being:

1. This method of marketing entails very high costs. To overcome this products must either be sold at very high margins, or have a very large turnover.
2. There are high associated administrative costs. With a single product or a small range, a large number of customers are required to make the venture economically feasible. This involves high clerical and office costs and there will be a proportionate increase in the number of debtors who have to be carried. The greater the number of customers, the more are likely to be in debt at any one time. Also bad debts are more likely because of limited local knowledge.
3. The distribution costs are likely to be high if a national coverage is required. This depends, of course, on the location of the manufacturing plants. The two major alternative forms of distribution applicable will be either using local stores and services, or else operating from one central point, which will entail high transport costs and consequently, time delays.
4. If the product has a seasonal demand, for example, seeds, fertilizers and sprays, there will probably be a seasonal work-load problem.

2. *Sales through agricultural merchants*

An alternative available to the manufacturer is to distribute through an agricultural merchant. Merchants are an established part of the agricultural industry, and specialist consideration will be given to their function in the final chapter. Again there are advantages and disadvantages accruing to the manufacturer who markets through an agricultural merchant. Included in this general term are agricultural dealers and requisite co-operatives, anything which fulfils the merchanting function of wholesale trading in agricultural requisites.

The potential advantages include:

1. Sales force requirements are reduced or eliminated.
2. Use is made of the merchants' local knowledge and contacts.
3. Clerical costs will be reduced because the merchant is responsible for the customers' accounts, producing less problems with finance and accounting. The manufacturers' financial dealings will be with the merchant.
4. Transport, storage and distribution will be easier, using the storage space of the merchant. It must be noted, however, that there is a growing trend, even with sales through the merchant, towards delivery direct to the farm, especially for goods of large bulk.
5. The use of the merchant can reduce the problems of seasonal demand for the manufacturer's product.

Conversely, the possible disadvantages of trading through an agricultural merchant can be summarized as follows:

1. The manufacturer has less control over the marketing effort. There will be an uncertain level of active selling. Manufacturers attempt to overcome this by representatives' promotion courses, however, the effect can never be definitely ascertained.
2. The merchant may be selling more than one range of product at the same time.
3. The technical product knowledge of the merchant's representative may be lacking.
4. There will be considerable problems with launching new products. It may well be difficult to persuade merchants to take on new products, and test launches will be very difficult; also there will be considerable difficulty in receiving accurate customer reactions and feedback.

In the United Kingdom a number of agricultural merchanting businesses have been purchased by manufacturers, particularly of animal feeding-stuffs. In this situation it is possible to combine some of the features of direct selling and marketing through an agricultural merchant. The result is an increased level of control over the marketing effort, typically with an increased variety of products reducing the importance of seasonal peaks. Also, the local knowledge and contacts of the merchants taken over can be utilized.

3. *Commission agents*

Commission agents are independent selling agents who carry the products of a manufacturer, selling on a percentage or flat-rate commission basis. The potential advantages and disadvantages of this, to the manufacturer, are as follows:

(a) *Advantages*

1. Use can be made of the existing sales contacts of the agent.
2. The motivation of the agent is usually good, because his rewards are directly related to his sales.
3. There are no overhead selling costs accruing to the manufacturer.

(b) *Disadvantages*

1. The manufacturer has no control over the sales effort.
2. Agents usually demand a relatively high margin, compared to those incurred with wholly controlled sales.
3. There may be problems associated with the limited product knowledge of the agent.

4. *Farmer buying groups*

Farmer buying groups are another alternative available to the manufacturer. The principles underlying buying groups are outlined in Chapter 8. They tend to be used as a complement to other methods of distribution. Again there are associated potential advantages and disadvantages:

(a) *Advantages*

1. A group concentrates a large number of small orders into a large one.
2. Payment is usually more prompt than with individual buying.
3. By working through the group secretary/agent it may be possible to increase contact with individual farmers.

(b) *Disadvantages*

1. Not all farmers are members of groups, therefore they cannot be used exclusively. Also groups tend to be poorly regarded by merchants and co-operatives. Dealing with a group may upset a manufacturer's relationship with his merchants.
2. The major factor stimulating sales tends to be price. As a result

low margins are likely, and therefore, after-sales service and related work cannot be undertaken.

3. There is less customer loyalty in groups than is common with other sales channels.
4. The biggest farmers tend not to be members of groups.

The most important products sold through groups tend to be those requiring little or no after-sales service, for example, tyres, batteries, wellington boots, veterinary products, tools, and basic machinery.

5. *Direct mail*

Direct mail can be considered as a means of marketing to the farmer. Its major attraction is that there is a very low cost of establishing customer contact, and there is also complete control over the marketing effort. However, there will probably be a need for some back-up sales force which will increase distribution costs. Transport costs are also high, particularly if bulky products are sent by mail. There are also associated accounting and finance problems, and there are, typically, low response rates, usually of about one per cent.

The terms of trading must be watched very closely, cash on delivery definitely being the most preferable. Direct-mail selling is used mainly for low bulk, one-off products with a high product appeal, and very little need for after sales service.

It may be possible to make use of fixed circulation, or specialist publications in order to elicit a better response. Direct mail is usually used to supplement other methods of marketing. For example, a glossy circular may be sent out advertising a product; the manufacturers' agent or representative would then be expected to continue the sales effort.

6. *Miscellaneous methods*

There are three other methods of distribution which are of some importance in the agricultural supply industry. These are:

(a) *Agricultural shows*

Agricultural shows are usually used for one-off sales or low bulk products, such as veterinary medicines. Otherwise shows are mainly for demonstration purposes and regarded as a public relations effort. Like direct mail selling, agricultural shows are normally a supplement to the main sales effort.

(b) *Selling in conjunction with providing a service*
This type of selling tends to be restricted to a very limited range of agricultural products. The majority of merchants selling soil additives such as lime and basic slag, for example, offer an associated delivery and spreading service. Similarly, mobile farm mill and mix units mill the farmers own cereals, and provide proteins, concentrates, and the mixing service.

(c) *'Directed' selling*
This occurs where the selling of a product is recommended as part of a contract. Some agrochemical manufacturers, and merchants, for example, offer herbicide and pesticide sprayers to farmers on very favourable terms, in return for a commitment by the farmer to purchase an agreed amount of the manufacturers products over a given period of time. Similarly, fertilizer manufacturers may offer to farmers pallet fork lift attachments for tractors on very favourable terms, in return for an assurance from the farmer that he will purchase an agreed amount of fertilizer over a certain number of years. The commitment may not be very tying. One major UK fertilizer manufacturer, for example, offers a farm management service. All farmers who avail themselves of this service sign a contract agreeing to purchase some of the output of that manufacturer over the next 5 years, however, no set tonnage is specified.

Distribution channels used in major farm requisites markets

The importance of these various distribution channels varies amongst the requisites purchased by the farmer. Seven product markets will now be considered; feed compounds, fertilizers, seeds, agrochemicals, farm machinery, farm buildings, and animal health products, and the major distribution channels used in each will be analysed, identifying any likely future changes in importance. The data on which the analysis is based has been produced as a result of a combination of personal research by the author and trade information sources.

1. *Feed compounds*
The compound-feeds market supports manufacturers of vastly differing sizes, from small village compounders, to large scale international companies with multi-million pound turnovers.

The largest national compounders tend to distribute their output through agricultural merchants and farmers co-operatives. In some cases the merchants of animal feeds have diversified into the supply of a large number of agricultural inputs, principally seeds, fertilizers, and sprays. Agricultural co-operatives, in addition to handling the output of national compounders, also, in certain cases, manufacture feeds themselves. This enables them to provide a balanced service for their farmer members.

The smaller compounders, co-operatives included, tend to sell direct to the farmer. In general they produce a limited range of lines, and may supplement their supply by purchasing extra lines from national compounders.

In the early 1970s it appeared that the national compounders were likely to achieve a complete domination of the market. This has not occurred, in fact the nationals are having considerable difficulty in holding on to a current market share of about 44 per cent, despite their making great efforts to rationalize and achieve a better customer relationship. The smaller compounders are taking full advantage of their better customer contact, and are often able to offer a price advantage. Regional compounders are likely to be particularly successful in dairying areas if they specialize in a limited number of dairy compound-feeds offered for bulk delivery.

The next few years are therefore unlikely to produce any major changes in distribution methods. The national compounders have now acknowledged that there are no large scale profits to be gained from agricultural merchanting. They do, however, have the advantage of having a broad capital base in a very capital-intensive industry, particularly in connection with the purchase of milling capacity.

2. *Fertilizers*

Three distribution channels are open to fertilizer manufacturers. They can:

(i)   sell directly to farmer customers;
(ii) sell through an independent agricultural merchant, which may well be an agricultural co-operative; or
(iii) sell through their own merchanting subsidiary.

All UK manufacturers have adopted a dual approach, with the greatest tonnage being sold through agricultural merchants. Almost three-quarters of all agricultural merchants handle fertilizers.

Agricultural merchants are therefore of very great importance to fertilizer manufacturers. Selling campaigns must be concentrated through the merchant's representative, which can be a limiting factor; complex programmes and gimmicks do not, in general, go down well.

Traditionally, fertilizers have been one of the less profitable lines which the merchant carries, hence usually they have been traded at a relatively low margin to keep the commodity moving. In order to stimulate trade, manufacturers provide technical representatives to back up the sales effort, although direct selling is not allowed. All orders must be placed through the local distributors' agent.

Co-operatives move a significant tonnage of fertilizer, however, they tend to be regarded with suspicion by the national manufacturers because of their willingness to buy up 'job lots' of fertilizers, particularly from abroad, if they can obtain a price advantage for their farmer members. The growing significance of buying groups should also be mentioned in this context. In the 1960s small groups of farmers were able to obtain discounts from manufacturers by bulking up their purchases. The national companies put a stop to this practice, however, recently national buying groups have again entered the field of bulk purchasing. They now purchase a very significant tonnage, often packed in their own bags and distributed to their farmer members.

Over the next few years the major change in the distribution channels used by fertilizer manufacturers is likely to be either an increase in the importance of buying groups, or, their total demise, if the major manufacturers join together to freeze them out, as they did with the smaller groups in the 1960s. There is also likely to be an increase in the importance of bulk deliveries of fertilizers, reducing transport costs, so long as the basic problem of moisturization can be overcome. If bulk deliveries do increase this would increase the importance of direct selling, and reduce the significance of merchant outlets. Otherwise, because of their heavy commitment to the merchants, the major manufacturers are likely to find it difficult to radically change their distribution channels.

It would appear that the major manufacturers have opted not to deal in the market fringe commodities, principally liquid fertilizers, organic fertilizers, and foliar feeds. This leaves a market gap for the smaller compounders to exploit, and is likely to ensure their continuing existence for the near future. The fringe markets are unlikely to compete with mainstream fertilizers. It is estimated that liquid fertilizers now have 10 per cent of the market, however, this is likely to be the limit of their growth, mainly because of storage problems.

3. Seeds

The agricultural seeds market comprises three major sectors; cereal seeds, herbage seeds, and fodder seeds. Cereal seeds are specific in that the farmer can, to a certain extent, meet his requirements by using seed from the previous year's arable crops. This possibility does not occur with herbage and fodder seeds.

In the UK about one-third of cereal seeds requirements are met from farm stocks, and the other two-thirds are provided by seed distributors, of whom there are a large number, varying considerably in size and importance.

Seed companies tend to provide a complete range, and there are four main categories of firms in the market:

(i)   national seed specialists, producing and marketing their own seed range;
(ii) franchise holders, large producers marketing brands through independent companies;
(iii) wholesale packers, not actually producing seeds, but procuring them in bulk, bagging up, and selling on;
(iv) traditional, small scale merchants, producing their own seed, bagging and selling it, typically with a turnover of less than 1000 tonnes per annum.

At the present time trade sources suggest that national specialists control about 60 per cent of the market, franchisers 10 per cent, wholesale packers 5-10 per cent, and small merchants also about 5-10 per cent.

New varieties of seed are very costly to produce, and the length of life is uncertain, depending on its resistance to disease. This is particularly appropriate to cereal seeds; herbage and fodder varieties tend to enjoy a greater longevity.

Once again there are three important distribution channels available to seed producers. Seeds are a traditional commodity handled by about 80 per cent of agricultural merchants. The traditional pattern was that the vast majority of merchants prepared their own seeds mixtures. Now this is far less common; however, a strong core of specialist seeds merchants survive, operating on a county or a regional basis, producing their own house grass ley mixtures, second generation cereal seeds, and so on. In this way national and regional seed specialists market their seeds on their own behalf. Alternatively, they can sell through the merchant trade, providing seeds for the firms which no longer produce in their own right.

The final possibility is, once again, to sell through agricultural co-operatives. Farm Seeds Federal is an amalgamation of 18 UK co-operatives, and is in the position of market leader, at least so far as the cereal seeds market is concerned. Other co-operatives which handle seeds are likely to buy basic cereal seeds from seed producers, other than Farm Seeds Federal, multiply them up on contract, and then sell them on to their farmer members. Overall, therefore, the influence of farmers' co-operatives in the marketing of seeds is very strong.

Seeds are also sold through commission agents, although this distribution channel is not used to any great extent in the industry. Commission agents handle seeds, on behalf of the smaller producers usually, in return for a commission on their sales.

Seeds are a commodity with a high profit potential making them of considerable interest to growers. In the future there is likely to be a decrease in the number of seed producers because of stringent EEC regulations. There is also likely to be an increase in the importance of the stake of co-operatives in seed marketing, and a marginal increase in the importance of nationalized seed specialists. Such growth could well result in the demise of a number of small-scale seed distributors, squeezed out by the rapidly escalating cost structure of the industry.

4. *Agrochemicals*

The major producers of crop chemicals predominantly use agricultural merchants as the distribution channel through which they dispose of their output. There is only one major manufacturer in the UK which sells direct to the farmer, serving about 10 per cent of the market. An alternative to these two methods is to sell via an agricultural contractor, however, this is of very limited importance in the total market.

Trade sources indicate that over 80 per cent of agrochemicals are sold via agricultural merchants. Crops chemicals are not a traditional line carried by merchants, the utilization and development of sprays on a large scale being a comparatively recent phenomenon. As a result, the approach of merchants to the handling of sprays is considerably different to their methods of selling other agricultural requisites. There is a large number of manufacturing companies to buy from, all constantly jockeying for a position in the market. Some merchants have supplied crop chemicals as requested by customers, using several different manufacturers, and have obtained the makers advice as and when it is required.

The selling of chemicals is often left to the general salesman to fit in with his other lines. However some merchants have appointed specialist salesmen with a greater technical knowledge of the products which they are handling. There has also been a trend towards the setting up of specialist spray merchants, particularly in arable areas. No merchant will deal with only one manufacturer, because by so doing they would be unable to offer a full range of services to the farmer. Even the merchants which are owned by manufacturers handle competitors lines.

Similarly, the one national firm which sells direct to the farmer markets not only its own crop chemicals but also those of its competitors, in order to be able to offer a full service. Because of this direct selling involvement, a large number of sale representatives are employed. The other UK manufacturers employ technical representatives, who back up the merchant's representatives with technical advice.

Sales through agricultural contractors tend to be relatively unimportant as a total part of manufacturers marketing strategy. Contractors apply specific types of spray in general, and seem unlikely to increase in importance in the future, mainly because farmers are required to spray crops at very short notice, so that it may not be possible to obtain a contractor.

Agrochemicals is the newest market among agricultural requisites, and it is also the one with the fiercest competition among manufacturers. For this reason the optimum choice of distribution channel is of great concern in the industry. In the future the importance of direct selling is likely to increase. This is a direct result of the increasing complexity of the products which are on the market. Because of this the sales representative is in a position of some authority with the farmer, which must be maintained. This will be achieved most effectively if the manufacturer has direct contact with its sales force rather than having to deal with merchanting intermediaries.

5. *Farm machinery*

The two major distribution channels used for marketing farm machinery are direct sales to the farmer and sales through agricultural merchants. In general, large, high value machinery is sold only through merchants, often known as dealers, and smaller machinery may be sold either directly to the farmer or through the merchant.

All tractor manufacturers, and combine harvester manufacturers sell through appointed agents. Different manufacturers have different policies with regard to the appointment of agents, however, all exercise some control over the operation of the merchants who handle their produce. The vast bulk of the market, by value, is, therefore, controlled by agricultural merchants. All tractor manufacturers tend to have an associated line of agricultural implements which they insist on their agents carrying. One multi-national manufacturer, for example, sets their UK main distributors a target number of tractors to sell, and according to the type of farming predominant in the area, associated targets for sales of implements manufactured by the company. This gives the merchant a financial inducement to sell the manufacturer's equipment in preference to competing lines which he may also be carrying.

Other agricultural machinery dealers exist without main distribution agencies. These firms operate by selling smaller implements which tend to have a higher margin of clearance. This enables the small merchant to undercut the main dealer who has to carry much larger overheads and therefore cannot take a smaller margin on his sales.

There are two major types of agricultural machinery dealers, the traditional, private, family businesses and the larger public companies, in certain cases farmer's co-operatives. The trend is very much towards the larger scale business to the exclusion of small firms. This is occasioned by the vast increase in the cost of machinery, increasing the capital requirements of running the business without any corresponding increase in the returns available to the firm.

There has been evidence of an increase in the importance of large-scale agricultural machinery dealers operating through a large

number of outlets, over a wide area of the UK. The major manufacturers reacted with alarm to this threat, because of the increased
bargaining power of the larger units, and have introduced various
schemes to control the size of their agents. One major manufacturer, for example, has laid down an edict that their agents must
not buy up a machinery dealer located within 100 miles of the
border of their trading area.

Sales direct to the farmer tend to be restricted to low value items,
which require very little back-up servicing. Some firms combine
direct selling and selling through an agricultural merchant, and
obviously in a situation like this problems can arise if the prices
charged vary widely. Overall, direct sales are of little relevance in
the market.

Another sector of the industry is machinery repairs. This service
tends to be supplied by two sources. Agricultural machinery dealers
usually provide a repair and maintenance service for their customers, and there also exist a number of specialist agricultural
engineers. Services in this sector are provided directly, with very
little advertising undertaken and firms tend to live on their repu-
tations. With spiralling costs, farmers have tended to carry out 'on
farm' repairs themselves, however, there are certain tasks which
require specialist attention and this should ensure the maintenance
of the machinery repair industry at, at least, its present size over the
next 5 years. Within this time period the change which is most likely
to occur in the distribution channels used by farm-machinery
manufacturers is the total demise of the private farm-machinery
dealer, driven out by the escalating cost structure of the industry.
These dealers are likely to be replaced by public companies expanding their trading areas, in some cases by direct takeover. There will
also, almost certainly, be a move towards exclusive distribution
franchises by the major machinery manufacturers in the future.
Further reference will be made to this in the next chapter.

6. *Farm buildings*

The farm buildings market is unique, among the farmer's requisites
being considered, in that all of the participants in the market use
the same distribution channel, namely, sales direct to the farmer. In
a market situation such as this the manufacturer's representative
has a very important role to play, since he is the major link between
the firm and the farmer. The representative usually acts in an

advisory capacity, and may well design the building which the farmer has in mind.

Personal research by the author suggests that price is an important factor in the market. For the purposes of qualifying for farm capital grant aid, all farmers must obtain two or three quotations for the cost of the building. In this way any discrepancies between manufacturers' prices are clearly shown up.

The impact of the Farm and Horticultural Development Scheme (FHDS) is of relevance here. FHDS is a long term scheme introduced as part of the Common Agricultural Policy, with the aim of improving the structural efficiency of farm holdings. To qualify for relatively high rates of grant aid, covering farm buildings among other things, farmers have to draw up a 5-year development plan showing that at the end of this time period the farm will be operating at a more efficient level than it is at the present time. This has had the effect of lengthening the farmer's planning horizon, and creating a more certain demand for new farm buildings.

There is extensive advertising of farm building services in farming periodicals in the United Kingdom. In general the representatives of the building firm spend a large proportion of their time advising on the planning and design aspects of potential custom. There is very little high pressure selling, and farmer loyalty to contractors shows itself by the large number of repeat purchases.

Looking to the future, there are unlikely to be any moves away from selling directly to the farmer. Because of the structure of the industry no other distribution channel seems appropriate, although one possibility may be that, given the growing importance of requisite co-operatives, it may be feasible for a farm-buildings manufacturer to build up a link with the co-operative, as a recommended supplier, offering a small discount to members of the co-operative.

7. *Animal health products*

Animal health products comprise an important, but relatively uncharted, part of the farmer's requisites market. The market for health products has grown considerably over the last few years, occasioned, mainly by two factors.

1. A tremendous improvement in medical knowledge relating to animal health, replacing unscientific medicines with products produced as a result of veterinary research.

2. An increase in stocking density, and the associated intensification of animal production, placing animals under increased
stress and producing a growing demand for animal health
products.

Because it is a relatively new market, and because of the nature
of its products, the distribution channels used for animal health
products are unlike those of any other farm requisite. Pharmaceuticals have traditionally been associated with veterinary science
and Government legislation now limits the supply of certain animal
health products to approved veterinary practitioners. Manufacturers of these products must, therefore, distribute them through
the veterinary profession. This now accounts for about 20 per cent
of the market. Non-restricted pharmaceuticals are sold mainly
through agricultural merchants and co-operatives, or else through
agents, normally operating on a commission basis. There are also
a number of instances of manufacturers selling direct to the farmers, although only one UK manufacturer does this on a large
scale.

Personal research by the author suggests that at the present time
an increasing number of farmers are introducing organized preven-
tative-medicine techniques to the management of their businesses.
In this way they agree, with their veterinary surgeon, a sum per
animal to be paid each year, regardless of the number of call-outs
which may occur. The veterinary surgeon is responsible for any
routine animal-health treatment and will come to the farm on call
whenever he is required. In this way the market for animal health
products is likely to become more organized in the future.

The next few years will almost certainly produce a continuing
growth in the demand for animal-health products. So far as the
distribution channels used by manufacturers are concerned the
major trend is likely to be an increase in the number of products
which can be supplied only through veterinary practitioners, as
a result of an increasing awareness of the dangerous side-effects
of certain products.

Factors of relevance to an orderly marketing of farm inputs

Given the size of the market for farm inputs it is a feasible notion
that a farmer can improve the efficiency of his purchase decisions

through the use of marketing management principles. There are a number of closely-interrelated factors which can be combined, and these will be considered now.

Financial control is probably the most important aspect of any orderly approach to the marketing of inputs so far as all farmers are concerned, since without money, or at least the necessary collateral to obtain it, it will not be possible to continue trading. A balanced and orderly cash flow is an essential prerequisite for an organized marketing of farm inputs.

The relative importance of cash flow tends to be related to the farming system. Established dairy farmers, for example, cushioned by the guaranteed arrival of a monthly milk cheque tend to have less of a cash flow problem than arable farmers, whose cash inter-flows depend entirely on their cereal yields, and their skill and/or luck in disposing of the final product. With interest rates of borrowed money reaching extremely high levels in recent years, cash flow has taken on a new dimension among all farmers. The aim, fairly obviously, with an orderly marketing of farm inputs is to co-ordinate, so far as is possible, the sale of finished products and the purchase of, or payment for, necessary inputs, so that at all times the amount of money which is borrowed from the bank is kept to a minimum.

With thought and planning, it is possible for such a system of marketing to reduce the requirements for borrowed money quite considerably. It is necessary, in this respect, to consider the seasonality effect on purchases of different products.

Certain products must necessarily be purchased fairly regularly throughout the year. The dairy farmer, for example, will have a reasonably constant requirement for concentrates to supplement the diets of the dairy cows, with perhaps an increased demand in winter months. Similarly, a pig producer will require regular supplies of feeds for his animals, unless he operates on a self sufficient mill and mix basis. Where regular purchases are made, possibilities exist for drawing up a preferential trading contract with a feeding compounding firm, at favourable rates, in return for a regular commitment to purchase.

For other inputs, requirements tend to be within a more restricted time band. Fertilizers, for example, are by and large required between March and September as a growth stimulant for grass and cereals. Fertilizer manufacturers would obviously prefer to be able to sell constant amounts throughout the year to reduce storage requirements and labour problems. To encourage a more balanced demand they offer a variety of deferred payment schemes, encouraging the farmer to take out of season delivery in return for long-standing credit, or cheaper prices. The farmer who takes advantage of this marketing opportunity is, therefore, able to fit in the payment for quite an important aspect of his farming programme at a time when his cash flow is best able to stand it.

The farmer who purchases his inputs in advance in this way must be able to store the fertilizer, and must also have worked out in advance his likely requirements. This to a certain extent limits his freedom of choice in decision making; however, in practice it is not a major problem. Seeds, herbicides, and pesticides are also required at fairly restricted times of the year. Similar possibilities exist, as for fertilizers, to organize the purchases, although not to the same extent.

Machinery purchases tend to be fairly capital intensive, certainly for larger items such as tractors and combine harvesters, suggesting a need for co-ordination once again, with cash flow. It is usually considered best to buy at a time when it is possible to get immediate usage from a machine, for example, not many combines are sold in October; however, in certain cases buying out of season may prove financially beneficial.

Small purchases tend to be made on a fairly *ad hoc* basis with little marketing forethought. Obviously, for commodities such as these the capital outlay is much less extensive, and stock control is the most important factor, making sure that there is a constant supply available to meet demand requirements.

For all of his purchases the farmer usually has alternative buying methods open to him. The simplest method would be for him to buy something by himself and pay cash on the nail for it. This very rarely occurs in agriculture, and the following are some of the more important alternatives.

1. Use of buying groups which undertake bulk purchases of a very wide variety of farmers' requisites, at favourable discount rates, enabling them to sell on to farmers at favourable prices.
2. Credit availability. All farm inputs can usually be purchased on credit, and traditionally merchants' credit was the most important source of finance in agriculture. Trade sources suggest that this has

now been surpassed by bank borrowing, and is regarded as an expensive means of borrowing. However, it is still used to quite a large extent. The norm for credit is usually 28 days from receipt of the invoice; there is a tendency for this period to be reduced as far as possible by offering discounts and so on.

3. Use of hire purchase and leasing. This is mainly applicable to machinery inputs. Hire purchase is regarded as a very expensive source of finance, not to be used except as a last resort; however, leasing of machinery is becoming a more realistic concept as machinery values have soared. Leasing separates the use of capital equipment from the ownership, distinguishing it from contracts such as a mortgage or hire purchase agreements where the user either has the ownership from the start, or has the option to acquire it.

4. A further possibility is the purchase of machinery through machinery syndicates. Through sharing the machinery the farmer reduces his capital outlay, and can obtain a cheap form of credit through syndicate credit companies.

5. Purchases of inputs through co-operatives. The principle here is that if the farmer purchases his requirements through a co-operative of which he is a member he will often receive the advantage of a dividend on his purchases, as well as contributing to the success of the co-operative.

It is apparent that so far as the marketing of farm inputs is concerned the most important aspects are the financial considerations. In spite of this, marketing cannot be subordinated to financial management, but must retain an independent role; for there are times when in purchasing farm inputs purely financial consideration will suggest that a purchase should not be made, while more wide-ranging marketing considerations will indicate otherwise. In selling, as in buying, the farmer can exist without consciously making any marketing decisions; however, in both situations possibilities exist for the farmer to improve his management and increase his profitability by a marketing-orientated approach to the purchase of his inputs and the sale of his finished goods.

11. The role of agricultural merchants in the supply of farm inputs

Classification of agricultural merchants

Throughout this book great emphasis has been placed on the diversity of British farms in their operations and in the degree to which they may either specialize in one type of enterprise, or else spread their activities over a number of different types of farming. This diversity is matched by the organizations which are generally grouped together under the title of agricultural merchants. Businesses range in size from one-man businesses with a very small annual turnover to regional and national organizations with multi-million-pound annual turnovers. Merchants may similarly specialize in the supply of one type of input to the farmers, alternatively they can provide a range of farm requisites, and in addition some merchants handle the output of farmers, trading in grain, potatoes, hay, straw, eggs, and so on.

No detailed classification of merchants has ever been undertaken to differentiate between, for example, agricultural merchants and agricultural merchant compounders as distinct from animal health distributors and fertilizer distributors. In the absence of any information identifying the totality of agricultural merchants along these lines, such a classification is impossible. In fact the information provided might be less meaningful than is often suggested because in many cases specialization in one product market is only a part of an individual merchant's operation and may mean nothing more than that the merchant has chosen to develop a degree of expertise in that particular area.

In the absence of a census of agricultural merchants it is difficult to obtain an accurate indication of the number of outlets operating in the United Kingdom. There are, however, two major trade organizations representing the interests of agricultural merchants and the majority of outlets are members of one or other of them.

Their membership returns, therefore, give a guide to the number of merchanting outlets.

The British Agricultural and Garden Machinery Dealers Association (BAGMA) had 553 members in 1979, with a total of 839 outlets.† They estimate that they represent 85 per cent of agricultural machinery dealers, which would make the total number around 990 outlets. In addition they have 98 members who specialize totally in the repair of agricultural machinery. In terms of numbers of people employed, their agricultural members employ, in total, about 30 000 staff.

The UK Agricultural Supply Trade Association (UKASTA) represents the manufacturing and distribution interests of firms involved in the merchanting of a wide range of agricultural commodities, principally feed compounds, seeds, grain, agrochemicals, and fertilizers. In 1979 a private survey indicated that they had a membership totalling 875, with a very great range in the size of businesses represented. Forty-one per cent of the membership, for example, employed less than 20 men, whilst 8 per cent employed between 100 and 1000 men, and one per cent employed over 1000 men. The small scale employers were mainly general merchants and the larger firms mainly specialist feed compounders.

The location of distribution outlets is very much related to the type of farming carried out throughout the UK. Agricultural machinery and agrochemical distributors are predominant in arable areas such as the East of England, while compound feeds and animal health product distributors are located mainly in livestock areas such as the North West of England. Distributors of fertilizers and seeds are located fairly consistently throughout the UK, reflecting their general demand by farmers of all types.

The number of distributing outlets which an area will support depends on various factors:

(i)   the number of farms in the area;
(ii) the size of those farms;
(iii) the type of farming most common in the area;
(iv) the total potential for trade (closely related to the type of farming);
(v)   economies of scale in distribution.

---

†The author is indebted to Mr J. Swift of BAGMA, for the information provided.

General experience suggests that there is very little relationship between the number of merchants and number of farms, with a very wide range between counties. Potential trade is a much more important factor. In low potential areas there are not only fewer merchants but they must also trade over a bigger area.

On the whole, the incidence of merchants is independent of the number of farms in the locality, and independent of the agricultural acreage. A much better relationship is given by the intensity of farming, as measured by the Ministry of Agriculture, Fisheries, and Food standard man-day per acre definition. In non-intensively farmed areas, merchant turnover will fall and distribution costs rise, resulting in lower profitability.

Trade areas for particular merchants are hard to define. Business can often be carried on outside the normal area because of personal connections, or a long-standing customer may move away and continue trading. Also a new salesman may bring his existing customers with him. The completely independent, smaller distributors tend to work closer to home, and rely on close personal relationships for the bulk of their trade.

The importance of farmers co-operatives in agricultural merchanting

Farmers requisite co-operatives play an important role in the marketing of the majority of agricultural inputs. In Britain, the co-operative share of the requisite market has traditionally lagged behind those of other countries, however, that share increased substantially during the early 1970s. In 1968, 15 per cent, by value, of requisites were purchased through farmers' co-operatives and by 1974 this had increased to 25 per cent. From then until the present time the total market share has stabilized.

Foxall (1978) provides a detailed analysis of the growth of co-operative trade in various requisite markets, illustrated in Table 11.1.

Although in the case of feeds the expansion of co-operative trade does not match that of the market as a whole, the situation is different for the other commodities, with co-operative trade expanding more quickly than the total market. The figures presented in Table 11.1 are of value only when considered in relation to Table 11.2, which gives the market share held by co-operatives over the same time period.

Table 11.1. Growth of selected agricultural product markets
and co-operative business from 1973 to 1976 (1973 = 100)

	1973	1974	1975	1976
Feeds				
Total market	100	120	120	164
Co-operative business	100	123	124	151
Seeds				
Total market	100	122	148	229
Co-operative business	100	131	181	264
Fertilizers				
Total market	100	139	152	176
Co-operative business	100	134	156	177
Machinery (inc. repairs)				
Total market	100	114	142	163
Co-operative business	100	123	147	176

Source: Foxall (1978).

From Table 11.2 it can be seen that the general pattern is one of stability. After the rapid expansion of the early 1970s, requisite co-operatives now appear to be holding their own against other suppliers.

Table 11.2. Co-operative percentage market shares
in the UK from 1970 to 1976

	1970	1973	1974	1975	1976
Feeds	13.0	16.9	17.5	17.6	15.7
Seeds	9.1	10.3	11.1	12.6	11.9
Fertilizers	18.5	19.1	18.4	19.6	19.2
Machinery	6.6	10.4	11.3	10.8	11.3

Source: Foxall (1978).

The role of co-operatives varies according to the requisite markets being considered. In the market for compound feeds, co-operatives play a dual role, as manufacturers selling direct to their farmer members, and as distributors of the output of national manufacturers. As producers, co-operatives have a limited role to play since they usually do not have the capital base to enable them to install milling capacity capable of producing a total range of products. Normally they produce a limited range of popular lines supplemented by the product range of a national compounder. Even West Cumberland Farmers (WCF), the largest co-operative in the UK, with a turnover in excess of £126m per annum, produce only part of their feed requirements and purchase the balance from a national compounder.

It is generally accepted that the co-operatives' productive share of the UK feed market is likely to double over the next 20 years to one fifth of a total market of around 13 million tonnes. Over the same period a number of national companies could withdraw from the market. Already there are examples of co-operatives pulling out of agreements with national compounders and beginning to compete directly with them. In 1977, for example, SCATS, Hampshire's biggest co-operative, ended its main dealer arrangement with BOCM—Silcock, and now produces in direct competition.

The number of regional and county compounders is also likely to decline, either going out of business, or being swallowed up by the remaining national compounders. Those remaining are likely to integrate, setting up direct links with the livestock industry. Overall, therefore, the importance of co-operatives in the feed-compounds market is likely to increase markedly.

Co-operatives also play a very important part in the distribution of seeds. According to trade estimates, Farm Seeds Federal (FSF), comprising 18 agricultural co-operatives is in the position of joint market leader, with over 11 per cent of the market. FSF operate as a non-profit making organization, any surpluses being distributed to the constituent co-operatives of the federal. This gives FSF a competitive advantage. It is likely that the co-operative share of the seeds market will increase in the future. Up to the present time, FSF have been very strong on the production side of the business, but have lacked marketing expertise. Since it would appear that they are now attempting to right this imbalance they should achieve even greater market success in future.

Co-operatives do not undertake the production of any fertilizers; however, since they distribute almost one-fifth of the output of the market, once again they have an important role to play. Farmers' buying groups should be mentioned in this context, as farmers buying together should be able to achieve a competitive advantage in the market, as long as their purchases are properly organized. Some co-operatives stock two lines of fertilizers. WCF, for example, carry two lines as part of a declared policy of offering their members a choice of brands. This creates problems so far as the manufacturer is concerned, but if co-operatives are regarded as being a desirable distribution outlet, then the situation must be accepted.

Marketing management problems facing agricultural merchants

There are various problems which affect the marketing management of agricultural merchanting businesses. The majority are of importance mainly because of the small profit margins which are characteristic of the industry. There are six major areas which will be considered in turn: communications, staffing, deciding what to sell, inventory decisions, credit, and transport facilities.

1. *Communications*

Initially the management of the merchanting business must set the objectives of the firm. This may be done either consciously or unconsciously. It is often difficult to communicate these objectives to the other members of the business. Properly-informed representatives are crucial to the success of the firm, since they have the responsibility of carrying out the objectives with the farmer customers. To a large extent this depends on the structure of the business, which is an essential element of the communications structure. Experience suggests that there are great differences within the industry, particularly between large and small scale merchants.

2. *Staffing*

The control and training of staff is a central management problem facing agricultural merchants. There have been various simple ratios produced to ascertain optimum levels of staffing. These ratios link the number of staff employed to the turnover of the business, or to particular parts of it. In reality such ratios are only of limited value, because of individual circumstances and changing market conditions.

A major staffing problem is related to the relative merits of sales staff who specialize in particular aspects of the business, as opposed to all-round representatives. The latter have the advantage of being able to deal with all aspects of the business required by an individual farmer, however, with the increasing complexity of various requisite markets, especially agrochemicals and animal health products, the specialist salesman has the advantage of being able to give more detailed advice to farmers who may well be intensively involved in one particular enterprise.

3. *Deciding what to sell*

Over time most merchant businesses have arrived at a range of requisite commodities which they provide for their farmer customers. The extent of the range varies considerably between businesses, and there is a central management problem of how to decide upon the range of commodities to be sold. Most decisions involve simply continuing existing lines, or else introducing slightly updated versions of them.

Detailed costing procedures can be used to ascertain the relative returns from different aspects of the business, however, many of the costs cannot be differentiated.

Major policy decisions, typically resulting in increased specialization, or a movement into a commodity not previously handled, must of necessity be based, to a certain extent, on intuition. Future market conditions can never be predicted exactly, and almost certainly never will be in the future.

4. *Inventory decisions*

There are two major management prolems related to inventory decisions: the types of stocks to carry and the associated levels. The makes of commodities which are sold vary little over time. Most merchants have long-standing connections with manufacturers, which are only broken as a result of major dissatisfaction on either part. A much more important aspect of management control is deciding the level of stock to carry. The two important aspects of this problem are the length of time the stocks will last and the cost of maintaining stocks. Most agricultural requisites have a long shelf life, with the exception of compound feeds which must be moved reasonably quickly to the farm after they have been produced.

Although other inputs will keep indefinitely, they have high associated costs, and, the cost to the merchant of holding stocks must be considered in relation to the desirability of being able to fill an order immediately it is placed. Most farmers place great importance on being able to obtain quick, if not immediate, delivery of requisites, making the holding of certain stock levels essential. The important factor, so far as the merchant is concerned, is not to hold excessive stocks, and this can be best ensured by extrapolation of demand levels in previous years, coupled with likely future changes. Care must also be taken to ensure that the cost of holding stocks is covered in the price at which the requisite is finally sold.

On the whole the cost of holding stocks is very high throughout the agricultural distribution industry and is resulting in the demise of the private distributor. Individual operators do not have the capital base to operate on the low returns to capital invested which are characteristic of the industry. Consequently multi-national and national business interests, such as RHM and Dalgety, are acquiring an increasingly important part of the market. National manufacturers who have moved to buy agricultural merchants in order to secure distribution outlets now realize the extent of the costs involved.

5. *Credit*

Credit provision is a management problem of critical importance in agricultural merchanting. All major purchases in the industry are invariably made in the expectation of short term credit provision, however, all merchants must decide how much credit to offer and for how long.

Traditionally British farmers have expected to be able to obtain extended credit facilities from merchants, and this situation worked without too many problems in times of low interest rates on borrowed money. In consequence, merchants' credit was a very important aspect of farmers' financial management, with credit being extended not just for 28 days but, on occasions, for a period of months. Merchants are now less able to stand credit until harvest, for example, when they would be repaid with a load of barley or wheat. Consequently, the interest rates associated with merchants' credit have become so high as to reduce the inclination of farmers to make use of the facility, and merchants are now very strict on credit extension. The majority offer their customers a 5 per cent discount for prompt payment, and have significant penalty clauses to discourage late payment.

Merchants customarily invoice monthly, in arrears, and farmers have until the end of the next month to pay the bill. This can create significant cash flow problems for the merchant, and one way to reduce this is by the introduction of split month accounting principles. One simple method of doing this is to invoice half of the merchants customers in the middle of the month, and the other half at the end of the month. Although both groups still receive the same length of credit, the cash inflows are more balanced throughout the month, reducing the relative indebtedness of the merchant.

Another important consideration is the credit worthiness of customers. The local knowledge of the merchant's representative is invaluable in relation to this. Farmers who are unable or unwilling to pay on time are a mixed blessing to a merchant, and are in general best avoided because of the consequent problems.

6. *Transport facilities*

A final, but important, management decision is related to the transport facilities which are provided by the agricultural merchant. In most cases the provision of some sort of transport fleet will be essential, since farmers tend to expect a delivery service as part of the price which they pay for the requisite. There have been various trends in the types of vehicles used by agricultural merchants, chiefly taking the form of increasing size of capacity. However, the majority of businesses have to provide at least one small capacity vehicle to service customers who are located in remote and inconveniently situated areas.

Transport costs usually comprise a major part of the cost structure of the agricultural merchanting business, and hence they are a major management concern. Various considerations affecting the costs of transport should be borne in mind. Maintenance is an important aspect, with the two major alternatives being either to provide internal facilities, or else use independent facilities. Most businesses have their own services in order to minimize the time which the fleet is off the road.

Idle time is of great importance to the merchant as the transport fleet is only of value when it is moving, but some standing time will be unavoidable, either at the merchants' premises or else on the farm. This must be taken into account when the optimum size of transport fleet is being considered. The planning of the transport operations is of very great importance. If at all possible neighbouring farms should be serviced together so that empty running should be minimized.

One possibility which could be considered is to hire a transport fleet rather than undertaking deliveries personally. This reduces the cost of delivery, but introduces uncertainty regarding the reliability of the service provided. For certain requisite commodities, manufacturers provide a transport service direct to the farm, however, delivery is more often the responsibility of the merchant, and hence of major concern to him.

Trends in agricultural merchanting

One important trend which must be considered is the impact of product linkages and own-produce branding in the marketing of agricultural requisites. Historically, the marketing of agricultural requisites has been undertaken using traditional and conservative methods. Because of this, up to the present time there is little evidence of use being made of product linkages by manufacturers in an endeavour to stimulate demand. There are isolated examples of fertilizer manufacturers providing handling equipment and management expertise, and agrochemical distributors providing equipment, however, these are very much the exception rather than the rule. The major reason for this is the traditional reluctance of the farmer to accept linkages because of a fear of being tied to a long term agreement which may prove to be to his disadvantage.

Even where a manufacturer operates in more than one major requisite sector, each product sector tends to operate individually. At one time a major UK manufacturer which operates in the fertilizer and agrochemicals markets combined the marketing effort for the two commodities. However, they reverted very quickly to separate operations. Although combined operations along these lines certainly involve technical, as well as sales and marketing problems, it is unlikely that these are insurmountable.

The lack of development is unfortunate, because product linkages are a feasible means by which manufacturers could stimulate demand for their output. Bulk buying is becoming increasingly popular among domestic consumers, and could be readily applied to farmers' inputs. The impetus would have to come from agricultural merchants, since few manufacturers would be in the position to offer, for example, a composite batch of fertilizers, agrochemicals, and seeds. Farmer acceptance would be the key factor, but it is possible that with a new generation of younger, more 'educated' and broad-minded farmers coming through, product linkage concepts

210   *The role of agricultural merchants*

will play a more important part in the marketing of agricultural inputs in the future.

Similarly own-product branding has become a more important aspect of the marketing of farmers requisites in recent years than it was traditionally. This varies by commodity, for compound feeds own-product branding is becoming increasingly important with increased advertising by manufacturers based on an identification of particular brand names. For agrochemicals, own-product branding is also becoming widespread as a number of the original products come off patent and are available to a larger number of manufacturers. The only way in which an identical product can be identified is by name, hence the growing importance of branding.

To a certain extent farmers 'see through' own-product brands, realizing that identical products are being offered under different names, and therefore reducing the effectiveness of the ploy. In the fertilizer market, for example, it is common knowledge that a wide range of varieties are produced by one manufacturer under different brand names. In general farmers buy very much on price and reliability. In a recent survey of 165 farmers (Foxall 1978), information was gained concerning the reasons given by farmers, for choosing their sources of supply. The results are given in Table 11.3.

Table 11.3. UK farmers' reported reasons for choice
of source of supply of agricultural requisites

Reasons	Percentage of responses
Economic advantage	61
Convenience	31
Loyalty to distributor	3
Loyalty to brand	2
Service	2
Dividend from co-operative	1
	100

Source: Foxall (1978).

The overriding influence on buyers' decision making is clearly economic advantage. In addition 'convenience' cannot be divorced from 'economic advantage' since it involved a reduction in the costs of transportation. Brand loyalty was not significant to any great extent.

The financing of the market for agricultural requisites is also of relevance, being of crucial importance chiefly because of the diversity of the industry. Certain individual requisites cost up to £20 000 and distribution outlets are expected, if not to hold stocks, at least to be able to obtain supplies very quickly. The financing of agricultural merchants is regarded as being perhaps the most important aspect of the business, and the approach to financial trading varies among the requisite commodities.

In compound feeds, for example, the national compounders invoice their distributors for payment on the fourteenth day of the month following delivery. Since the distributor will invariably be working on 28 days credit to his customers, the merchant is in the position of standing credit to the farmer. This can only be overcome by ensuring that the price charged to the customer covers the cost of providing credit. In a highly competitive market this is not achieved easily.

In the agricultural machinery industry there are two major methods of payment utilized by the major manufacturers. One method lays the cost of financing credit firmly with the machinery dealer, and the other places the cost with the manufacturer. One major manufacturer, for example, invoices its dealers immediately supplies have left the factory gates, and payment is required within 7 days. To extend the credit period, it is possible to take out a 3 month Bill of Exchange, on which interest is payable at 3 per cent over finance house base rate. The cost of credit is, therefore, paid for by the dealer.

The alternative method is for the manufacturer to provide his distributors with extended interest-free credit on machinery supplies. Any machinery sold within the time period must be paid for immediately it is sold, and the balance must be paid for at the end of the time allowed. The length of time allowed extends to 6 months in one instance in the UK. The cost of credit, therefore, lies with the manufacturer and the aim is to encourage dealers to stock more machinery.

For machinery with seasonal demands, balers for example, manufacturers offer extended credit to stimulate out-of-season buying. One manufacturer, for example, offers credit on baler purchases until the next season of usage.

Agricultural machinery dealers make their profits from the discount offered to them by manufacturers. Tractors usually carry a discount of 18 per cent (some of which will be passed on to the farmer as an inducement to buy). For smaller machinery the typical system is that dealers are given 5 per cent discount if they pay for goods within 30 days, with perhaps a higher discount for out of season goods, and in addition buy at a 20 per cent discount on recommended retail price, with an extra allowance for bulk purchases.

The range of services required in the agricultural supply industry is also an important factor which should be considered, and can be divided into two major aspects, services required by the distributors from the manufacturer, and those required and/or expected by the farmer from the merchant. In both cases credit provision is one consideration which comes immediately to mind, this has been referred to previously in the chapter.

In addition to credit there are two further aspects to the manufacturer/distributor relationship. Distributors, by and large, require and receive advice from the manufacturer, particularly when a new product is introduced. This is necessary since the distributor cannot be expected to develop an expertise in all of the many commodities which he is likely to carry. For this reason the majority of manufacturers employ technical representatives, a major part of whose job is to act as a troubleshooter, advising distributors and final customers on a wide range of aspects of the manufacturers' products.

There would appear to be a definite move towards exclusivity in certain parts of the supply industry. This is where the manufacturer requires his distributor not to sell competing products. Personal research by the author indicates that the trend is particularly important in the agricultural machinery market at the present time, and is beginning to become more relevant in the feed compounds market. Exclusivity is common in the seeds market, but is unlikely to become of any significance in the markets for crop chemicals and animal health products because of the nature of the products offered. No manufacturer offers a completely comprehensive range in either market, resulting in open competition.

There are other services required by farmers from distributors. In addition to credit facilities, farmers also expect to receive free advice from their distributors, even if this does not result in a sale being made. Often the provision of advice can be both time consuming and costly for the distributor. Fertilizer distributors, for example, will be required to undertake soil analyses, at their cost, which may or may not result in a sale. The distributor's representative plays a very important advisory role, hence the selection of representatives, and their training, is crucial. Wrong advice can prove very costly to the reputation of the distributor.

Management advice is usually expected by farmers, particularly with feed compounds, animal health products, and crop chemicals markets. Again this must be provided by the distributor and is reflected in the price charged for the product. One service which must be provided by farm machinery distributors is that of providing a machinery repair facility, and holding stocks of spare parts. Repairs cost the distributor money as virtually all workshops are unprofitable. There are very high overheads, in terms of both skilled labour and expensive machinery. It is also necessary to provide a field repair service during harvest periods. The provision of spare parts can be profitable, although a good storeman is critical, avoiding the two perils of overstocking and understocking. At any one time a medium-sized distributor is likely to be holding up to £250 000 worth of spare parts, at its own expense. Ability to supply spare parts, replacements, and/or service can be crucial to a farmer's choice of machinery brand, particularly for machines which have short, seasonal, but intensely busy usage periods.

Likely future changes in the structure of agricultural merchanting

The structure of agricultural merchanting, as with all industries, is in a continual state of flux. Radical changes are most likely to occur in two major product areas. These are feed compounds and farm machinery. In both markets there will almost certainly be moves towards rationalization of outlets, although for very different reasons.

In the feed-compounds market rationalization is already occurring and has been occasioned by increasing costs of haulage, and the swing away from imported cereals to those grown in the United Kingdom. New mills are being built on country sites in livestock areas, where the demand for animal feeds is greatest, leading to the decline of the traditional port mills. The new mills are also much more efficient in terms of productive capacity per man employed, furthering the decline of established mills. In 1979, for example, BOCM-Silcock opened two new mills in the UK with annual productive capacities of 4000 tonnes of feed per employee, double the capacity of their existing country mills, and four times that of their port mills.

The new mills will also be very heavily bulk-orientated. One national manufacturer, for example, opened a new mill in 1979 which produces only bulk feeds. Over the next 20 years it seems probable that the industry will move completely over to bulk feeds with only speciality lines, such as horse and rabbit feeds, sold in bags. The result is likely to be that in future bagged feeds will command a price premium of up to 25 per cent. In addition, distribution areas are likely to be closely controlled with over 80 per cent of sales within a radius of 25 miles of the mills.

Transport costs and the cost of building new mills will be the factors governing the actions of manufacturers in the future. In view of the high cost of putting up new mills, or modernizing existing facilities, this is likely to prove prohibitive for smaller compounders without access to large cash funds. A number of manufacturers may be forced to go out of business if they are unable to compete in efficiency terms, since lower production costs will be used to undercut prices in the highly competitive market which is developing. The competition is so intense because the existing productive capacity in the United Kingdom is already about 2 million tonnes in excess of current demand. Mills need to run at around 60 per cent capacity in order to break even, and this factor is likely to become increasingly important, with the cost of building new plant now at about £30 per tonne of capacity.

In the market for farm machinery, rationalization is likely to occur because of the escalating cost-structure of the industry. Prices and manufacturing costs have increased drastically over the past 10 years, and the result, so far as the agricultural machinery dealer is concerned, is that the overheads associated with the business are extensive. As a result of the high degree of competition among machinery dealers, profits are low.†

---

†Trade sources suggest that a 10-11 per cent gross clearance on turnover is common, leaving a net profit of 2-3 per cent of turnover.

Because of these factors, private machinery dealers are likely to be squeezed out of the market, taken over by public companies or large company interests capable of spreading the overheads over their assets. There is evidence of an increase in the importance of machinery dealer chains; one major dealer, for example, has some 30 branches over a wide area of the United Kingdom, however, these are viewed with misgivings by manufacturers because of the potential countervailing power which could be applied by the dealers. For all this, dealer chains, and larger businesses are likely to increase in importance in the future.

The action by tractor manufacturers in moving towards the granting of exclusive franchises to dealers is likely to increase the rationalization of the industry. In the past, dual franchises have been common in the market, with dealers selling the competing lines of two manufacturers. This will almost certainly come to an end over the next 5 years. One of the largest UK manufacturers, for example, gives a reduced discount to dealers who hold a dual franchise and even those manufacturers who had a policy of selling to anyone, are now moving towards sole franchising. The major reason for this move is defensive, as a result of the increasing importance of overseas competition. The result is likely to be that some small dealers will be left with the unprofitable franchises, another factor likely to lead to a decline in their importance.

In the markets for other agricultural inputs there are unlikely to be any radical changes. The agricultural merchanting trade has gone through radical changes over the past 20 years, with an industry-wide rationalization of outlets.

The number of agricultural merchanting outlets has declined dramatically in the United Kingdom over the last 15 years. The author estimates that in 1979 there were approximately half the numbers of outlets compared to 1966. There are various reasons for this decline in the number of outlets. Some of the more important are:

1. The level of profitability in agricultural merchanting has been low, particularly when farmers incomes were under severe pressure in 1969-72. The fortunes of the two sides of the industry are very closely linked.
2. The average age of merchant business owners has been relatively high and a number of firms have closed when the owner retired.

References

Alexander, R. S. (1960). *Marketing definitions: a glossary of marketing terms.* Compiled by the Committee on Definitions of the American Marketing Association, Chicago.

Allen, G. R. (1958). *Agricultural marketing policies.* Blackwell, Oxford.

Barker, J. W. (1980). Opportunities for direct farm sales. *J. Univ. Newcastle Upon Tyne agric. Soc.*, **XXVII**, 24-8.

Barker Report (1972). *Report of the committee of inquiry on contract farming.* HMSO, London.

Baron, P. J. (1978). Why co-operation in agricultural marketing? *J. agric. Econ.* **XXIX**, 109-18.

Bateman, D. I. (1972). In *Marketing management in agriculture.* University College of Wales, Aberystwyth.

—— Kerr, A., Owen, R. E. and Thomas, T. H. (1971). *The structure of livestock marketing in Wales.* University College of Wales, Aberystwyth.

Beaumont, J. (1971). The cost of processing and distributing food in the United Kingdom. *Econ. Trends* **217**, 1.

Bowbrick, P. (1979). Evaluating a grading system. *Ir. J. agric. Econ. rur. Sociol.* **7**, 117-26.

—— and Twohig, D. (1977). *Pick-your-own fruit marketing,* Economic Research Series, No. 22, An Foras Taluntais.

Britton, D. K. (1969). *Cereals in the United Kingdom: production, marketing and utilisation.* Pergamon, Oxford.

Brooman, F. S. (1971). *Macro-economics.* Allen and Unwin, London.

CCAHC (1978). *Agricultural co-operation—a policy review,* CCAHC.

Chivers, J. and Kirk, J. H. (1967). *Market price intelligence for dessert apples.* Report Number 1. University of London, Wye College.

Cobbledick, R. H. (1974). *Pick your own harvesting.* Ministry of Agriculture and Food Factsheet 74-087, Vineland, Ontario.

Cochrane, W. W. (1958). *Farm prices, myth and reality.* University of Minnesota Press, Minneapolis.

Colley, R. H. (1961). *Defining advertising goals for measured advertising results.* Association of National Advertisers, New York.

CSO (1980). *Annual abstract of statistics, 1980 edition.* HMSO, London.

Ezekiel, M. J. B. (1938). The Cobweb theorem. *Q. Jl Econ.* **52**, 255-80.

EEC Commission (1977). *Forms of co-operation between farms for production and marketing in the new member states.* EEC Commission, Brussels.

Fabian, M. S. (1972). *Pick your own marketing—selected information and bibliography.* Department of Agricultural Economics and Marketing, University of New Jersey, New Brunswick.

Fox, K. A. (1951). Factors affecting farm income, farm prices, and food consumption. *Agric. Econ. Res.* **III**, 65-82.

Foxall, G. R. and McConnell-Wood, M. M. (1976). *Member society relations in agricultural co-operation.* Report No. 22. University of Newcastle upon Tyne, Department of Agricultural Marketing.

Foxall, G. R. (1978). In *Yearbook of agricultural co-operation*, Plunkett Foundation, Oxford.

Galbraith, J. K. (1967). *The new industrial state.* Hamish Hamilton, London.

Heller, R. (1972). The myopic marketing myth. *Marketing*, September, 32-5.

Home-Grown Cereals Authority (1978). *Weekly Digest*, **4**, 4.

Hughes, R. (1969). In *The Sunday Times*, 20 April 1969.

Josling, T. E. (1973). In *Britain in the E.E.C.* (ed. D. Evans) pp. 95-8, Gollancze, London.

Kaddar, T. (1975). *Selling or marketing agricultural produce?* Third Ami Shachori Memorial Lecture.

Kempner, T. (ed.) (1976). *A handbook of management.* Penguin, London.

Kimber, R. G. (1977). In *Yearbook of agricultural co-operation.* Plunkett Foundation, Oxford.

Kohls, R. L. (1968). *Marketing of agricultural products.* Macmillan, London.

Kotler, P. (1972). *Marketing management, analysis, planning, and control.* Prentice Hall, Englewood Cliffs, NJ.

Levitt, T. (1962). *Innovation in marketing.* Pan Books, London.

Linlithgow Report (1924). *Departmental Committee on Distribution and Prices of Agricultural Produce.* HMSO, London.

McCarthy, E. J. (1971). *Basic marketing: a-managerial approach.* Irwin, Homewood, Il.

McClements, L. D. (1970). Note on harmonic motion and the Cobweb theorem. *J. agric. Econ.* **XXI**, 141-6.

MAFF (1980). *Household food consumption and expenditure: 1978.* The Annual Report of the National Food Survey Committee. HMSO, London.

MAFF (1978). *U.K. food and farming in figures.* HMSO, London.

Marsh, J. S. (1977a). *Int. Affairs* **53**, (4), 604-14.

—— (1977b). *U.K. Agricultural Policy within the European Community.* University of Reading, Department of Agricultural Economics.

May, M. E. (1977). Generic advertising. *Oxford agrar. Stud.*, Vol. VI.

Metcalf, D. (1969). *The Economics of Agriculture*, Penguin, Harmondsworth, Middlesex.

Mitchell, G. F. C. (1975). *The influence of market intelligence on farmers livestock marketing decisions.* University of Bristol, Department of Economics.

MMB (1979). *United Kingdom Dairy Facts and Figures 1979*, United Kingdom Federation of Milk Marketing Boards, Thames Ditton, Surrey.

Moore, J. N. (1970). *Am. Fruit Grower* **84**, 39.

Moore, J. R. (1968). Bargaining power potential in agriculture. *Am. J. agric. Econ.*, 1051-3.

Morley, J. A. E. (1975). *British agricultural co-operatives.* Hutchinson Benham, London.

Rodger, L. W. (1971). *Marketing in a competitive economy.* Cassell/Associated Business Programmes, London.

Shaw, A. W. (1912). Some problems in market distribution. *Q. Jl Econ.* **26**, 703-60.

Shepherd, G. S. and Futrell, G. A. (1970). *Marketing farm products—economic analysis.* Iowa State University Press, Iowa.

Teichman, H. (1975). *Rent a tree.* Proceedings of Ontario Roadside Marketing Conference, Ontario.

Terpstra, V. (1972). *International Marketing.* Dryden, Hinsdale, Il.

Thomas, T. H. and Bateman, D. I. (1973). *Fat cattle prices in Wales.* University College of Wales, Aberystwyth, Department of Agricultural Economics.

Turner, E. S. (1968). *The shocking history of advertising.* Penguin, Harmondsworth, Middlesex.

Verdon Smith Report (1964). *Report of the committee of inquiry into fatstock and carcase meat marketing and distribution.* HMSO, London.

Viaene, J. (1977). Towards co-operation and concentration in the sale of agricultural products. *Rev. Agric* **1**, 94-107.

Working, H. (1960). Price effects of futures trading. *Food Res. Inst. Stud.* **1**(1), 3-31.

Zif, J. and Israeli, D. (1978). Objectives and performance evaluation of marketing boards. *Eur. J. Market.* **12**, 413-27.

Index